Unfailing Treasures

Devotional

Finding God's treasures along life's journey.

You can take it with you!

Lisa Buffaloe

Unfailing Treasures Devotional
© 2014 Lisa Buffaloe
Published by John 15:11 Publications
Updated 07242023
Visit the author's website at https://lisabuffaloe.com

All rights reserved. No part of this book may be reproduced or transmitted in any way, form or by any means, electronic or mechanical—including photocopying, recording, or by any information storage and retrieval system— except brief quotations in printed reviews. without permission of the author.

Scripture taken from the New Century Version® (NCV). Copyright © 2005 by Thomas Nelson, Inc. Used by permission. All rights reserved.

Scripture taken from the NEW AMERICAN STANDARD BIBLE® (NASB), Copyright © 1960, 1962, 1963 ,1968, 1971, 1972, 1973 ,1975, 1977, 1995 by The Lockman Foundation. Used by permission.

Scripture quotations marked (NLT) are taken from the Holy Bible, New Living Translation, copyright © 1996, 2004, 2007 by Tyndale House Foundation. Used by permission of Tyndale House Publishers, Inc., Carol Stream, Illinois 60188. All rights reserved.

THE HOLY BIBLE, NEW INTERNATIONAL VERSION®, NIV® Copyright © 1973, 1978, 1984, 2011 by Biblica, Inc.™ Used by permission. All rights reserved worldwide.

Scripture taken from the New King James Version®. Copyright © 1982 by Thomas Nelson, Inc. Used by permission. All rights reserved.

Scripture taken from *The Message*. Copyright © 1993, 1994, 1995, 1996, 2000, 2001, 2002. Used by permission of NavPress Publishing Group.

Scripture quotations marked HCSB are taken from the Holman Christian Standard Bible®, Copyright © 1999, 2000, 2002, 2003, 2009 by Holman Bible Publishers. Used by permission. Holman Christian Standard Bible®, Holman CSB, and HCSB® are federally registered trademarks of Holman Bible Publishers. Scripture marked ERV, Copyright ©2006 World Bible Translation Center.

Cover photograph by Lisa Buffaloe   Cover design by Scott Buffaloe
ISBN: 978-0692243503

~ *Dedication and Thanks* ~

To Jesus Christ, my amazing Savior, thank You for the unfailing treasures of Your grace, mercy, peace, joy, and love. Thank You for allowing me in Your family.

Thank you to my sweet husband and son for your love and encouragement. You are both such amazing blessings from the Lord!

Thank you to my friends, who wish to remain unnamed, who helped with editing and final preparations. You bless me abundantly! Your prayers and support have been such a wonderful source of encouragement. Thank you.

To my readers, thank you. Thank you for joining me on this writing journey. May we all enjoy the unfailing treasures of God's goodness and eternal love!

~ *Treasure Hunting* ~

Treasure is sought after, fought over, and pursued to the ends of the earth. The lure of riches drives people to risk and sacrifice everything. Yet no matter how much wealth is gained, nothing is safe from thieves, decay, or the fluctuating world economy, and not one penny can be taken beyond the grave.

I haven't yet met a person who doesn't treasure something or someone. The dilemma we face as humans is there isn't a transportable system beyond the grave. Yet I have good news! Jesus, The One who conquered sin, death, and the grave, offers eternal treasures you can take with you!

This amazing offer for unfailing treasures is secure, and transportable beyond space and time.

Satisfaction, love, joy, peace, comfort, and everything your soul craves, is offered for free and found in the presence of Jesus Christ. For in a relationship with Jesus, eternal life, joy in abundance, peace that passes understanding, and everlasting love is found. There is no better treasure than found in Christ.

God has granted marvelous access to His Kingdom through faith and trust in Jesus, and the treasures of heaven are available to all who believe. And while we remain here in this sometimes-messy world, God has blessed us with guidance for a joyful journey through His word. The Bible is full of treasures for each of us, and the more time spent in God's presence and in His word, the more abundant and beautiful the soul-jewels.

As we explore, I want you to know God deeper, to <u>really</u> know Him, to fall in love with Him as intensely as He is in love with you.

Will you join me in this hunt for unfailing treasure? Each devotion, whether short or long, will invite you to join in mining for treasure. As we ponder God's truth in His word, let's dig deep, and dive into the sweet refreshing river of living water to find the gold, silver, and pearls of great price.

Treasure is waiting. Seek and you will find. Happy seeking!

"Do not store up for yourselves treasures on earth, where moth and rust destroy, and where thieves break in and steal. But store up for yourselves treasures in heaven, where neither moth nor rust destroys, and where thieves do not break in or steal; for where your treasure is, there your heart will be also." ~ Matthew 6:19-21 (NASB)

~ *Joy for You* ~

May I speak to you? Yes, you. It's okay to be joyful. You have my permission in spite of your circumstances. Not that my permission is worth much, but I have it on good authority—the best authority—that it really is okay to be joyful.

Because in God's presence is fullness of joy. And we are told to count it all joy even when we're in trials. And to rejoice, and again we're told to rejoice. Jesus tells us that with Him we have joy and have it to the full. Oh, there are so many truths to joy, because The Truth is joy!

So today, my friend, my precious down-hearted friend, I'm sending you joy. Joy straight from heaven's throne to you. Joy wrapped in baby belly laughs, puppy paw high-fives, and smiling flowers.

Verses on joy are found throughout the Bible. And in those verses, we find joy that isn't just written as words, but joy to infuse every beat of our heart.

Joy is found in trusting God and loving Him. "Let all those rejoice who put their trust in You; let them ever shout for joy, because You defend them; Let those also who love Your name be joyful in You." ~ Psalm 5:11 (NKJV)

Joy comes from God and from praising Him. "I will be filled with joy because of You. I will sing praises to Your name, O Most High." ~ Psalm 9:2 (NLT)

Joy is found in God's presence. Setting God first brings joy. "I have set the LORD continually before me; because He is at my right hand, I will not be shaken. Therefore, my heart is glad and my glory rejoices; my flesh also will dwell securely. You will make known to me the path of life; In Your presence is fullness of joy; in Your right hand there are pleasures forever." ~ Psalm 16:8-9, Psalm 16:11 (NASB)

God's joy is greater than earthly prosperity. "Many people say, 'Who will show us better times?' Let your face smile on us, LORD. You have given me greater joy than those who have abundant harvests of grain and new wine." ~ Psalm 4:6-8 (NLT)

God's commands bring joy and insight. "The commandments of the LORD are right, bringing joy to the heart. The commands of the LORD are clear, giving insight for living." ~ Psalm 19:8 (NLT)

Joy comes through obedience. "I take joy in doing your will, my God, for your instructions are written on my heart." ~ Psalm 40:8 (NLT)

Seeking God brings joy and satisfaction. "The poor will eat and be satisfied. All who seek the Lord will praise him. Their hearts will rejoice with everlasting joy." ~ Psalm 22:26 (NLT)

"Joy is the gigantic secret of the Christian life." ~ G.K. Chesterton

Rejoice for you have a Savior that saves. Jesus is the Savior who wipes away all past sin and promises an eternal joy-filled home. So much joy to you!

"These things I have spoken to you so that My joy may be in you, and that your joy may be made full." ~ John 15:11 (NASB)

Mining for Treasure

As you read the verses on joy, which ones meant the most to you?

What does joy mean to you? Based on God's word, what do you think joy means to God?

God is a God of joy, and since you are created in His image, you are created by joy, in joy, for joy!

For further joyful mining, visit Psalm 21:6, Psalm 28:6-7, Psalm 30:11, Psalm 32:11, Psalm 33:1, Psalm 34:5, Psalm 34:8, Psalm 40:4, Psalm 40:16, Psalm 41:1, Psalm 43:4, Psalm 45:7, Psalm 46:4, Psalm 47:1, Psalm 51:12, Psalm 59:16, Psalm 63:6-7, Psalm 65:3-4, Psalm 65:8, Nehemiah 8:10, 1 Peter 1:8, and so many more.

Memorize joy verses, for they are promises of God's joy to you!

~ *If You Knew Me* ~

I was completely stunned by something that happened. Someone on one of my social sites unfriended me, someone I thought was close, who knew me and knew my heart. And I wondered why.

I'm definitely not perfect, and I know everything I do whether in private or public will be under scrutiny by God and man. So, every post, every tweet, every blog, everything I write, everything I do in my life, I pray and so try to honor God.

I wanted to tell my friend that if she really knew me, she wouldn't have unfriended me. I was so sad, so very sad, knowing that if only she knew my heart, she would know I care and cherish her friendship.

Then I realized I only knew a small part of the deep grief that God must feel in how we act and react to His offer of friendship and love.

The whisper in my soul prompted that if I really knew God, if I really trusted His heart, would I ever doubt His loving care?

And I'm so sorry. Oh Father, I believe, help my unbelief.

God's Spirit whispers...

If you knew Me, you wouldn't believe that lie.

If you knew Me, you wouldn't be worried.

If you knew Me, you would know
My heart is always good.

If you knew Me, you would trust Me.

If you knew Me, you would not be afraid.
If you knew Me, you would know
you can always believe Me.

If you knew Me, you would know
My plans for you are always good.

If you knew Me, you would know
I will never leave you or forsake you.

If you knew Me, you would know
My love is unfailing.

If you knew Me, you would rest.

If you knew Me, you would know
I will be with you forever, and ever.

If you knew Me,
you would never doubt My love.

I love you -- God.

Heavenly Father, I love You. Thank You for your kindness, patience, and unfailing love. Help me to know You more and love you more deeply.

Mining for Treasure

If we truly knew God how different do you think our lives would be? Will you take the time to get to know God by spending time reading the Bible and praying? Please know, always know, that He loves you!

~ *Seeking God's heart* ~

"I have found David the son of Jesse, a man after My heart, who will do all My will." ~ Acts 13:22 (NASB)

Why did God find David a man after His heart? Look at the beauty of David's Psalms and read about his desire and longing for The Lord. "As the deer pants for the water brooks, So my soul pants for You, O God." Psalms 42:1 (NAS)

Throughout the Psalms, David reveals that his desire for God was beyond anything this earth could offer. What great hope David's life should give us. His failings were as large as his faith, but one thing never changed -- his love and desire for God. "I will praise You, O Lord, with my whole heart; I will tell of all Your marvelous works. I will be glad and rejoice in You; I will sing praise to Your name, O Most High." ~ Psalm 9:1-2 (NKJV)

David was not perfect, but he was devoted and passionate to know, serve, and love God. "The Lord is my strength and my shield; My heart trusted in Him, and I am helped; therefore, my heart greatly rejoices, and with my song I will praise Him." ~ Psalm 28:7 (NKJV)

He committed terrible sins (adultery, murder) in his lifetime, but he always came back searching for the heart of God. "As for me, I said, "O Lord, be gracious to me; Heal my soul, for I have sinned against You." ~ Psalm 41:4 (NASB)

David's life should encourage each of us. We don't have to get everything right in our lives to be used by God, He does not require perfection. We don't have to be perfect; we serve a perfect Savior. And through His perfect love we find acceptance, mercy, and eternal grace.

Throughout history, God has used imperfect people in mighty ways. The great women and men of faith in the

Bible were human, complete with failure. Only Jesus lived a perfect life, and through Him God reaches out to us all.

I'm so grateful the Bible doesn't hide the failures of those who were used in mighty ways. The people God chose struggled with sin and the hardships of life. And yet even through their imperfections our mighty God did amazing things.

Is there something in your life you feel might keep you from being used by God? Take that thought, perhaps that sin, and talk to God. If you need to ask His forgiveness, please talk to Him right now.

God promises when we come to Him seeking His mercy and grace, He will forgive. And those sins are never to be remembered again by our loving God. Accept the treasures of His forgiveness. Seek God's heart and you'll find God's wonderful blessings filling your heart.

Mining for Treasure

Do you find strength that, in spite of failures, God can change your heart to have a heart like His?

Do you believe that if God can forgive David's sin's, He can forgive yours?

Take a deep breath. Even with your imperfections and failures, even with your struggles, God loves you and wants to fill your heart with His love.

Will you take a moment to thank God for His perfect love, to thank Him for His perfect grace and forgiveness?

~ *Look Back* ~

I've had reoccurring neck issues, and at times couldn't even glance over one shoulder without great difficulty. Driving was a challenge, but for the safety and well-being of everyone (including myself) I'd force my neck to turn to make sure I could properly see my surroundings. Checking to verify roads or lanes are clear and looking back is very important, and if not done properly disaster could happen.

God tells us to look back, to remember His faithfulness, to remember all the wonderful things He has done for us and for others. Unfortunately, many people tend to look back at everything negative, at every disaster, heartache, and hard thing they have gone through.

I'm not being flippant about the trials and suffering of life; God knows there are major difficulties. However, we need to remember to look back the right way, to see and remember and praise God for what He has done. We are to set up markers and memorials higher than the heartaches and failures; higher than it all, high enough for our gaze to see the eternal hope.

Look back and remember our God is a faithful God. Remember His rescues, remember the times He helped you through, remember His mercy and grace, remember His goodness, remember His unfailing love, and remember He will never leave you or forsake you.

Each time you look back, each time you remember, your strength will grow, your hope will rise, and your faith will stand stronger.

"He has made His wonders to be remembered; The Lord is gracious and compassionate." ~ Psalm 111:4 (NASB)

"Remember His wonderful deeds which He has done, His marvels and the judgments from His mouth." ~ 1 Chronicles 16:12 (NASB)

"I shall remember the deeds of the Lord; surely I will remember Your wonders of old." ~ Psalm 77:11 (NASB)

Mining for Treasure

Can you think of a time when in the midst of a trial you became aware of God's loving presence?

In what ways did He make His presence known? Was it through an answered prayer, the beauty of a sunset or perhaps through some loving words from a friend?

When you look back on your life do you see God's faithfulness and grace? Whatever your answer, please make the time to remember all the ways God has worked in your life. Reflecting on God's grace will give you faith and hope for the future.

~ *Pull Up!* ~

The Lord blessed me with a visual over this last year. As a blogger and writer, I spend much of my day alone. One day when wondering about this lone journey, God gave me a visual of being in the jungle, hacking through a trail with my machete (sword of the Spirit jungle style).

Although I'm alone on the trail, God is with me. I see and sense His presence, His smile, His encouragement. My friends are on their own paths. Some are traveling together, others are alone. And at times we see one another, shout greetings, smile, and then get back to work on our jungle pathways.

In the distance is a cliff. There is no bridge, but there is no fear. For when I reach the cliff, before I can even contemplate my next action, God swooped over as a huge white bird and gently grabbed me with His talons.

I am safe under His wings, and I soared and smiled in joy. Then we flew lower, so low my body was scratched on the branches of trees. However, I continued to laugh and enjoy the journey. Then the gentle whisper in my soul reminded me to pull up and I would not get injured. Ah, such simplicity. Pull up!

As I pondered these truths, I realized, it is in God's presence we find His joy. It is in His presence we find the guidance needed. It is in His presence we find all we need for every need. And even when life is hard, we can pull up under His wings.

So, whatever is happening, whatever you face, remember to always pull up under His wings.

Pull up! Because no matter where we are in our life, we can find joy as we pull up into God's presence. "Because You have been my help, therefore in the shadow of Your wings I will rejoice." ~ Psalm 63:7 (NKJV)

Mining for Treasure

Can you think of a time that God has rescued you or protected you from something?

How is God directing your paths or guiding you now?

Take time to read God's word, highlight or write down the verses that mean the most. Speak them verbally. For in speaking The Word, The Word gets further into our soul, pulling us closer to God's presence.

"You will make known to me the path of life; in Your presence is fullness of joy; In Your right hand there are pleasures forever." ~ Psalm 16:11 (NASB)

~ *Key to Freedom* ~

Just enough pain remained after my last surgery that I couldn't get comfortable or in a deep sleep. A nightmare came, and an evil force had me in its grasp; a demonic voice put ice in my veins. I was unable to scream, unable to break free.

But I knew Who I needed to call – **Jesus**. Finally, the name of Jesus formed in my thoughts. I woke gasping and sputtering the name of my Savior. Although out of the enemy's grasp, the darkness remained. I woke my sweet husband to join me in prayer. And I continued to say the name of Jesus, to whisper verses, and to pray for everyone the Lord brought to mind.

And as morning light came, I realized Romans 8:28 again showed the reality of God's truth. "We know that in all things God works for the good of those who love him, who have been called according to his purpose."

God turns what the enemy means for evil into good – EVERY time!

I don't imagine the evil attack was so I would pray for protection for an abundance of people. So, I'm smiling, because a nasty nightmare became a blessing of prayer, verse reciting, and praise.

Our Savior is like that, He turns around negative situations into something amazingly positive. We might not see how God is working in our present circumstance, but we can be assured, God is working everything out for good.

When you feel locked in by the enemy, remember to use your key.

Jesus is the key to freedom!

Mining for Treasure

Are you in a trial and longing to feel God's presence? What words of comfort might Jesus say to you during this trial?

Remember His promise: "And surely I am with you always, to the very end of the age. "~ Matthew 28:20 (NIV)

Whatever negative is happening in your life, turn around the mess the enemy sends by praying and praising God.

Keep your focus on Jesus, His name on your lips, and God's truth embedded in your heart, soul, and mind.

~ *The Addition That Leads to Subtraction* ~

For months I was blessed to study the book of James as I prepared for a speaking event. The evening I returned from the retreat, very unwelcome and unexpected news rocked our world.

James 1:2-4 continued to repeat in my thoughts. "Consider it pure joy, my brothers and sisters, whenever you face trials of many kinds, because you know that the testing of your faith produces perseverance. Let perseverance finish its work so that you may be mature and complete, not lacking anything." ~ James 1:2-4 (NIV)

Nothing was joyful in our situation, yet God's word gently beckoned to remember and consider God's provision, faithfulness, and unfailing love. And also, to consider how this new trial, this testing of our faith, would lead to a beautiful finish.

One translation of James 1:2 reads "count it all joy." As I remembered, considered, and counted God's faithfulness, the deeper the joy came and the deeper the peace.

The more our focus turns from the situation to focus on God, the bigger and surer the faith, and the smaller the problem becomes.

Count it all joy isn't just a "Don't worry, be happy" philosophy, it is life-giving, life-filling, joy-giving truth. When we add up all God is doing, and all He has done, all His amazing faithfulness, strength, mercy, grace, and love, the counting subtracts from the difficulties of the problems.

Count and add with gratitude, and you'll find the worries, fears, and problems are subtracted from your life. Count it all joy and you'll find God's joy!

Mining for Treasure

An old hymn titled, Count Your Blessing, advises to "count your blessings and see what God has done."

I wonder how often we forget blessings come in all sizes and shapes. It's easy to count the BIG blessings, yet overlook the blessings of our senses, of having God's Word, of being able to read, of the beauty in the world.

Blessings are all around, and the more we see the blessings, the more we count the blessings, the more our problems are subtracted from our life.

Start today by counting and adding your blessings.

~ *Treasure Guarding* ~

A relationship with God through Christ is the ultimate treasure. "Guard, through the Holy Spirit who dwells in us, the treasure which has been entrusted to you" ~ 2 Timothy 1:14 (NASB).

Are you guarding your treasure with your thoughts, actions, what you watch, what you read, what you say, and how you live? Read carefully the following warnings.

"Keep and guard your heart with all vigilance and above all that you guard, for out of it flow the springs of life. Keep my commands and you will live; guard my teachings as the apple of your eye.

"Guard your steps as you go to the house of God and draw near to listen. Be alert and on your guard; stand firm in your faith. Guard and keep [with the greatest care] the precious and excellently adapted [Truth] which has been entrusted [to you], by the [help of the] Holy Spirit Who makes His home in us." ~ Proverbs 7:2 (NIV), Proverbs 4:23 (AMP), Ecclesiastes 5:1 (NASB), 1 Corinthians 16:13 (AMP), 2 Timothy 1:14 (AMP)

Mining for Treasure

Are you guarding the treasure of you? Are you guarding your home and family?

The shows you watch on television, the movies you view, the reading material in your home, do they guard your thoughts and relationship with Christ?

~ Deeper Still ~

I have several friends who love diving deep into God's word. We strap on the belt of truth and plunge into the depths. With the Light of the World shining bright into the darkness, we submerge to discover more fully God's word. It's an awesome adventure!

Bible study isn't just about checking off we've read a verse or chapter.

Bible study is digging and tunneling to find treasure in God's word, it is the unearthing of true riches, not just for us, but to share with others.

Bible study is finding the treasure of God's heart.

So sweet friends, leave the swimmies on the shore. Open up your Bible and immerse yourself in God's treasures, where you'll find a deeper relationship, a deeper life, a deeper experience, a deeper existence, and deeper joy!

Go deeper still.

"Deep calls to deep... Praise be to the name of God forever and ever; wisdom and power are His. He reveals deep and hidden things; He knows what lies in darkness, and light dwells with Him." ~ Psalm 42:7, Daniel 2:20,22 (NIV)

Mining for Treasure

Will you pray with me? Heavenly Father, help me not be satisfied with skimming the surface. I want to dig deep, gathering wealth and jewels of Your truth, love, grace, and mercy to share with a lost and hurting world. Help me to burrow straight to the depths of Your heart!

~ *Fear or Faith?* ~

Every day we can choose to walk in fear or faith. Every moment we choose. I'll be honest, there are times when fear comes like a dark flood, darkening The Sonshine. And I gasp for the breath of the Holy Spirit. I strain to see the light of The One who is light.

When life seems so frail, cling to The Life. Run to The One who promises to guide the path, to give strength and courage. And although knees may wobble, choose to walk in faith on God's path and stay in His way. As the fires of life blaze, stand firm in The Living Water. Be confident as Paul, "For I know whom I have believed and am persuaded that He is able to keep that which I have committed unto Him against that Day." ~ 2 Timothy 1:12 (NKJV)

Our Savior lives. He rescues. He guides safely home. He has overcome the world. So "why am I discouraged? Why is my heart sad? I will put my hope in God! I will praise him again-my Savior and my God!" ~ Psalm 43:5 (NLT)

Hope comes when focusing on The One who is hope. Hope comes when the soul is knelt in thanksgiving and praise. Hope comes when remembering God's truth, "Have I not commanded you? Be strong and courageous. Do not be afraid; do not be discouraged, for the Lord your God will be with you wherever you go." ~Joshua 1:9 (NIV)

God is with us. Faith is fortified in the hope and knowledge that He will direct our paths. "You make known to me the path of life; you will fill me with joy in your presence, with eternal pleasures at your right hand." ~ Psalm 16:11 (NIV)

Mining for Treasure

Turn away from fear and turn toward faith. For no matter what the situation or what may happen in the future, God's perfect love is for you. And fear is always driven out by God's perfect love.

Choose faith in love that is perfect and love that loves you perfectly. Choose God who blesses with faith to walk in faith.

~ *The Prettiest Pot* ~

Years ago, my sister and I took pottery lessons. We listened as the teacher guided our feeble efforts to create something of beauty. When I say feeble, I mean disastrous.

No matter what we tried to create, the clay wouldn't respond to our prodding. And to top off our inadequacies, my sister and I became tickled. And the more we giggled, the more those around us responded with blank stares, which only made our situation all the worthier of side-splitting laughter.

We had planned on creating pretty pots or beautiful vases to sit on our shelves. What we took home were two stumpy little pots that looked more like ashtrays (and neither of us smokes). I still have my creation, which my sweet husband uses in the closet to store his spare change.

If clay had human properties, I would have told you our clay was very rebellious. It refused to be molded to our grand designs.

Yet don't we do the same thing with our Heavenly Father, the Master Potter? When we refuse God's touch and refuse to be molded by Him when the pressure of life comes, we lose His blessings and the beauty He is longing to create in us and through us.

The most beautiful masterpieces are created when the clay is soft and pliable. It is not outward beauty God desires, but the soul-deep beauty of a surrendered life.

Andrew Murray sums up beautifully, "What has God promised you, and what can God do to fill a vessel absolutely surrendered to Him? Oh, God wants to bless you in a way beyond what you expect. From the beginning, ear hath not heard, neither hath they eye seen, what God hath prepared for them that wait for Him. God has prepared unheard-of-things, blessings much more wonderful than you can imagine, mightier than you can conceive. They are divine blessings."

Mining for Treasure

How can you be soft and pliable in The Master's Hands?

Surrender to God's molding and let His blessings flow. You are treasure in an earthen vessel, let God unlock the treasure of you!

~ *Divine Protection* ~

During a time when my husband was in the hospital for a hip replacement, I needed to run home. The hospital halls and lobby were deserted, visitors had left and only the night shift remained. I called a friend to update her as I left.

Scanning the parking lot, an uneasy feeling caused me to walk as quickly as possible to the car. I opened the door, jumped in, and pressed the lock button. When I looked up, a man stood at the passenger window. He seemed to come from nowhere.

He waved to get my attention. I prayed for protection and asked my friend to hold on and not hang up. I carefully rolled down the window about an inch.

He said he had left the hospital earlier with his wife and new baby and had run out of gas at a certain street. He asked if I could take him to a station.

Uncomfortable and unfamiliar with the area, I asked him to check inside the hospital for help, and I quickly pulled away. My friend who had been listening, told me the street he mentioned was blocks away with many places to find help.

As I left the parking lot, I knew God had protected me. (I found out later the hospital where my husband was staying did not even have a labor and delivery department.)

During the forty-five-minute drive home, my mind was blurred by concerns and prayers for my husband. A gas station came into view, and I realized I had forgotten to fill the car and was almost on empty.

As I pulled into the pumps, I was painfully aware of the late hour and remote location. Praying for large angels to protect and surround me, I started pumping gas.

A few moments later a pickup truck pulled in slowly behind my car. Praying again, I glanced over to see three men sitting in the front of the truck. The one in the middle looked enormous. Even in the lights I could not see faces, they seemed covered in darkness.

I turned away, praying furiously as the driver stepped out and began gassing up.

Within only a few minutes, the driver put away the nozzle, jumped in his truck, and announced loudly to the others he had gotten enough gas. In a flash they backed out and drove away.

Relieved and grateful, I wondered what those men had seen. What angels might have been standing next to me?

That night you can be assured the praise and prayer session lasted until sleep overtook, because I knew whatever happened, with God's help it was going to be okay.

I'm not going to tell you if you pray hard enough, or have enough faith, you'll always be protected from evil and harm. This night all turned out well. But I've been through some rough times. In my earlier years I was molested by a baby sitter, raped by a doctor, stalked, chased by a man with a knife, drugged and locked up, and a bevy of other very unpleasant events. Life isn't always easy.

But one thing I can assure you, if God doesn't take you around a difficult situation, He will take you through. And God always takes what the enemy meant for evil and turns it into good.

Sometimes the rescue comes swiftly in hospital and gas station parking lots, and other times the rescue comes in the healing, renewal, and restoration.

Whatever happens God will be with you. And His Divine Protection will always, always, carry you through.

Mining for Treasure-

What paralyzes you, and why? How can you let that go today?

How have you seen God turn bad into good in your own life?

Do you long to experience perfect love, versus fear? Ask God for that today.

"Now, thus says the Lord, your Creator 'Do not fear, for I have redeemed you; I have called you by name; you are Mine! When you pass through the waters, I will be with you; And through the rivers, they will not overflow you. When you walk through the fire, you will not be scorched, nor will the flame burn you.'" ~Isaiah 43:1-2 (NASB)

~ Joy-Filled Friendship ~

Do you desire to be filled with the joy of the Lord? It's possible. Really! The joy of the Lord isn't just for the people who have the great lives, or those who stand in pulpits or have the titles or big ministries.

God's word promises, "...You will seek the Lord your God, and you will find Him if you search for Him with all your heart and all your soul." ~ Deuteronomy 4:29 (NAS)

And when we accept Jesus as our Savior and Lord, we are blessed with an intimate friendship. He says, "I no longer call you servants, because a servant does not know what his master is doing. But I call you friends, because I have made known to you everything I heard from my Father." ~ John 15:15 (NCV)

Jesus calls us friends. Wow. Oh my, amazing.

In God's presence is fullness of joy and Jesus is joy, and the Holy Spirit blesses us with joy as the fruit of the Spirit.

So that joy? That joy-filled friendship?

Put your hand on your chest. It's right there. If Jesus is in your heart, your heart has the joy and the sweet friendship of Jesus!

"I have told you these things, that My joy and delight may be in you, and that your joy and gladness may be of full measure and complete and overflowing." ~ John 15:11 (AMP)

Mining for Treasure

Rest joyfully in the truth that Jesus is your joy!

~ Needed ~

Just think, we are all needed, every single one of us. "The whole body depends on Christ, and all the parts of the body are joined and held together. Each part does its own work to make the whole body grow and be strong with love" ~ Ephesians 4:16 (NCV).

We all have a part and a purpose. I need you; you need me, we are all part of God's family. :)

Sometimes it's easy to think we are not needed or alone in the world. But just like a huge puzzle, every piece is needed.

Please always remember that you were created with purpose by our loving God. And as a Christian you are needed and loved in the beauty of your specific part in the family of Christ.

And the wonderful thing is, if you aren't yet part of the family, there is always room and love for more!

You are needed! Come on in, let's have a group hug!

Thank You Father, for Your family. Thank You that wherever we go and whatever happens, we will not be left without a connection to You. Keep my eyes and heart open to love and serve with Your love.

Mining for Treasure

Is there a spiritual family that God has blessed you with, perhaps a small group or the members of your church?

How does that spiritual family walk with you and show you the love of Christ?

How can you extend the love of Christ or in some way serve your spiritual family?

God wants us to belong to His family: "Yet to all who received Him, to those who believed in His name, He gave the right to become children of God-children not of natural descent, nor of human decision or a husband's will, but born of God. "~ John 1:12-13 (NIV)

If you have made that decision to believe in His name, celebrate that our loving and powerful God has made you part of His family...forever!

Remember no matter how insignificant or how unimportant you feel, you have a place in the body of Christ that is needed and appreciated!

~ *Fire Shine* ~

The other night I started thinking about what most people would classify as problems. You know that long list, the one where difficulties are compared? Mention kidney stones and you may hear about Uncle Ralph's kidney stone the size of a watermelon. And whatever you do, don't mention the childbirth experience.

My thought is this... what if problems are merely blessings in disguise?

Do you remember the story of the three Hebrew young men, Shadrach, Meshach and Abednego (See Daniel 3)? The king had erected a 90-foot tall golden statue of himself for all to worship. Anyone who did not worship the image would be thrown into a raging fire.

These young men refused. Here is their reply. "If we are thrown into the blazing furnace, the God we serve is able to save us from it, and He will rescue us from your hand, O king. But even if He does not, we want you to know, O king, that we will not serve your gods or worship the image of gold you have set up." ~Daniel 3:17-18 (NIV)

The king is furious, makes the fire seven times hotter and throws them in bound hand and foot. The king's command was so urgent and the furnace so hot that the flames of the fire killed the soldiers who took up the young men.

"Then King Nebuchadnezzar leaped to his feet in amazement and asked his advisers, 'Weren't there three men that we tied up and threw into the fire?' They replied, 'Certainly, O king.' He said, 'Look! I see four men walking around in the fire, unbound and unharmed, and the fourth looks like a son of the gods.'" ~ Daniel 3:24-30 (NIV)

They walked out of the fire unharmed, nothing was burnt, and they didn't even smell like smoke. The only thing that burnt away was the ropes that bound them.

And, an even better fact is, while they were in the midst of that raging fire they were not alone. They chose not to bow down to anything other than God even though they didn't know He would save them. They didn't hear God's voice or see His hand until they were thrown into the raging fire.

Are you in the fire? Look for God. He is with you.

The fire will burn away what binds you to this earth to free you for eternal joy. With God the negatives become positives. God has a plan–a perfect, awesome plan for your life.

Are you suffering? I know it's hard but rejoice. Paul tells us..." we also rejoice in our sufferings, because we know that suffering produces perseverance; perseverance, character; and character, hope. And hope does not disappoint us, because God has poured out his love into our hearts by the Holy Spirit, whom he has given us." ~ Romans 5:3-5 (NIV)

Watch for the by-products of suffering, for in God's hands even a lump of coal becomes a diamond. Know that hope comes, know that the suffering creates an eternal hope-filled shine.

Are you in the fire? Shine on, dear friend, shine on.

Mining for Treasure

Consider what happened to Shadrach, Meshach, and Abednego, then read the verse below from Isaiah 43.

"When you pass through the waters, I will be with you; and when you pass through the rivers, they will not sweep over you. When you walk through the fire, you will not be burned; the flames will not set you ablaze." ~ Isaiah 43:2 (NIV)

Whatever fire you may be facing in life, please remember that God will always be with you to carry you through.

~ *Yearning* ~

There is a soul-deep agony, a yearning, an overwhelming ache, that wells up inside, infusing every cell of my body. And yet this ache, I will not run from, this ache I long for and desire. It is a holy burn firing through every sinew and synapse, a longing so deep, so real, and so intense that nothing on earth can satisfy.

What is so desperately needed is found only in Jesus. Only He, The Word, can give words to my longing. Only Jesus can fill the hole in my soul and satisfy the whole of my soul. For it is He who formed me; He who made my soul.

The soul-stirring brings the soul to kneel at the amazing beauty of God's love. He who loves me, knows all about me (every sin of pride, envy, failure, every messy, so very messy embarrassing sin) and still loves me. Still.

And when that ache, splits wide-open with agony, the agony is infused with joy. His Spirit brings that longing, He calls. He calls to come home and yet bids me to stay. To stay and tell others about Him, tell others about His love, tell others that their overwhelming soul-ache can only find satisfaction in Him.

The soul kneels still, aching, longing to run to His arms. To go home. And yet, so many here I love – my sweet husband and sweet son, family, and friends who carry precious pieces of my heart.

And oh, how my heart would break if you were unaware of His love and chose not to come home.

God beckons to every soul to fill with His love, peace, forgiveness, and joy. Please don't miss the blessing -- the joyful, soul-filling blessing -- of being a follower of Jesus Christ. Through Jesus comes grace and mercy for eternity.

Please, please, please don't miss God's call; don't run from the ache, run to The One who splits open so that what is split wide can be filled, fully, completely filled with His love.

Mining for Treasure

Have you tried to fill that ache in your soul with something other than Jesus?

Soul-satisfaction, soul-fulfillment comes with Jesus. Take some time to sit at His feet and give Him every empty place of your soul. His filling is complete and wrapped in eternal love.

~ *Praise away the enemy!* ~

Don't ever discount the power of praise. Look closely at these two verses and notice what happened during praise.

"As they began to sing and praise, the LORD set ambushes against the men of Ammon and Moab and Mount Seir who were invading Judah, and they were defeated." ~ 2 Chronicles 20:22 (NIV)

"About midnight Paul and Silas were praying and singing hymns to God .... Suddenly there was such a violent earthquake that the foundations of the prison were shaken. At once all the prison doors flew open, and everybody's chains came loose." ~ Acts 16:25-26 (NIV)

Wesley L. Duewll writes of the power of praise, "Praise pierces the darkness, dynamites long standing obstructions, and sends the demons of hell fleeing."

When we praise, God's power is released!

When we praise, the enemy is routed!

When we praise, the prison doors open, and the chains fall off!

Whatever you are facing, whatever situation is in your life, remember the power of praise. Praise, praise, praise God!

Mining for Treasure

What situation are you in right now that makes you feel like it has you surrounded?

Can you bring this difficulty before the Lord and release your grip? Give thanks and praise to Him as you do.

Ponder this verse: "I will give thanks to you, Lord, with all my heart; I will tell of all your wonderful deeds. I will be glad and rejoice in you; I will sing the praises of your name, O Most High." ~ Psalm 9:1-2

Always remember, in the praise of our awesome God, you will find the awesome power of God.

~ What Football Taught Me ~

I enjoy American football. I enjoy the game so much my right knee required surgery to replace torn and destroyed ligaments and tendons. Over the years the injury progressed until there was no choice but to call the surgeon. Yet even with my scars, I still love the game.

The goal of football is to win by scoring points. When a team has possession of the ball, they must keep moving forward. Successful teams work together, they encourage one another. Whether by way of passing, running, or kicking, their focus stays on the goal to win the game.

Time is never stagnant. A team can't take as much time as they want, they can't squander time celebrating a good play or bemoaning a bad one. Whether they were champions or losers last season or last game, they keep moving forward to win the present game by focusing on the current play.

I'm learning those truths in my own life. If I sit and whine about what happened, or even dance victory dances over glory moments, I may miss today. I may miss how God is working now and where He is leading.

Paul reminds us, "Don't you realize that in a race everyone runs, but only one person gets the prize? So, run to win!" ~ 1 Corinthians 9:24 (NLT)

Keep moving forward. Keep your eyes on the goal. You're not running alone. You're not on the field of life without help. Jesus will never leave you or forsake you.

Encourage your teammates, cheer them on, remember as Christians we are on the same team.

So, keep moving forward, keep pressing in and pressing on, for at the end an eternal, amazing prize waits!

Mining for Treasure

Remember to stay in the game. Encourage those around you. You are not alone; God has a goal and purpose for your life. Keep your focus on Him, keep moving forward.

Who can you encourage today?

What glory moments or negative times have captured your attention?

Press into God and press on, for everyone in Christ will receive eternal rewards!

~ *Psalm 91 Beauty* ~

The other day, God beckoned me to read again Psalm 91. I love the verses, the truth that gives hope and security. And when I looked again with the Hebrew translations at my fingertips, I made notes of the definitions that stood out, that gave a deeper meaning, a new meaning, and a new truth.

Would you take a few minutes with me to look and consider the depth and riches of God's word? Oh my, you will be so blessed.

Psalm 91

He who **dwells** (*remain, sit, abide, have one's abode, to stay*) in the **shelter** (*covering, hiding place, secret place*) of the Most High will **abide** (*lodge, remain, dwell*) in the **shadow** (*protection*) of the Almighty.

I will say to the Lord, "My **refuge** (*trust, hope, shelter from rain, storm, danger, or falsehood*) and my **fortress** (*fastness, stronghold, castle, strong place, fort, defense*), my God, in whom I trust!"

For it is He who delivers you from the **snare** (*traps, plots, calamity, or source of calamity*) of the **trapper** (*bait-layer*) and from the deadly pestilence.

He will **cover** (*hedge, overshadow, protector, screen, weave together*) you with His pinions, and under His **wings** (*borders*) you may seek refuge (*flee for protection, to put trust in God, confide or hope in*); His **faithfulness** (*truth*) is a shield and bulwark.

You will not be afraid of the terror by night, or of the arrow that flies by day; of the pestilence that stalks in **darkness** (*gloom, spiritual unreceptivity*), or of the destruction that **lays waste** (*ruin, spoil, devastate*) at noon.

A thousand may **fall** (*fall away, fall short, settle, waste away, be cast down, fail*) at your side and ten thousand at your right hand, but it shall not approach you.

You will only **look on** (*pay attention to, consider*) with your eyes and see the recompense of the **wicked** (*ungodly, criminal, hostile to God, guilty of sin*).

For you have made the Lord, my refuge, even the Most High, your **dwelling place** (*habitation*).

No evil will befall you, nor will any plague come near your **tent** (*dwelling, habitation, sacred tent of Jehovah, tabernacle*).

For He will give His angels charge concerning you, to **guard** (*keep, protect, preserve, keep within bounds*) you in **all your ways** (*direction, path, course of life, of moral character*).

They will **bear you up** (*sustain, support, lift up, carry, assist, armor bearer*) in their hands, that you do not **strike** (*stumble*) your foot against a stone.

You will tread upon the **lion** (*wicked men*) and cobra, the young lion and the serpent you will trample down.

"Because he has loved Me, therefore I will **deliver** (*escape, bring into security, bring to safety*) him; I will set him **securely on high** (*inaccessibly high, too high for capture*), because he has known My name.

"He will call upon Me, and I will answer him; I will be with him in **trouble** (*distress, adversity, anguish*); I will **rescue** (*remove, withdraw, equip for war, equipped, make strong, brace up, invigorate, saved, set free, delivered*) him and honor him.

"With a long life I will **satisfy** (*filled, fulfilled*) him and let him **see** (*perceive*) My salvation."

Mining for Treasure

Reflect on Psalm 91. What did you notice as you read through the verses with some of the Hebrew translations? What stood out?

Are there any events or situations that God says He won't see you through?

Is there anything too difficult for Him?

Did you see a richer meaning for your life and the daily battles?

Since God fears nothing, you can rest fearlessly in our loving God.

Information compiled using Psalm 91 New American Standard Bible (NASB) and Hebrew translations from Lexicon: Strong's

~ *Keep Me Blazing for You* ~

"Since you are like lukewarm water, neither hot nor cold, I will spit you out of my mouth!" ~ Revelation 3:16 (NLT) Oh my, I don't want to be spit out by God!

I want to burn for You, Father.
Don't let my embers be scattered from busyness, complacency, or misplaced priorities.
Don't let me use the wrong kindling from the world instead of The Word.
During the howling winds of trials, keep my love clinging steady to Your grace.
During the rain of sorrow, keep my love protected by Your truth.
When life is so cold, keep my love pressed deep into the burning coals of Your power.
I want to fan into flame, kindle afresh, and keep my love blazing for You.
Heavenly Father, keep my soul blazing with passion for You!

"For this reason, I remind you to fan into flame the gift of God, which is in you through the laying on of my hands." ~ 2 Timothy 1:6 (NIV)

Mining for Treasure

To keep God's love burning in your heart, spend time in prayer, praise, thanksgiving, and reading His word.

~ Life Happens ~

Sometimes life brings joy, happiness, and dreams-come-true. Other times life brings tragedy and heartache. However, the true life, a life of joy, happiness, and dreams-come-true, comes to those whose life is hidden in Christ.

Regardless of the pain and suffering, life continues to bring life when life is coming through The One who is life.

There is stability and a never-ending, free-flowing, living-water life when we realize as Christians, we truly do receive a happy ending. Whatever happens here on earth is only temporary. Whatever the enemy means for evil WILL be turned into good for those who love God and are called according to His purpose. (Romans 8:28)

Our calling, our existence, is more than what we can fully see here on earth. Our life was birthed with meaning and purpose.

We are each created for fellowship with the Maker of the Universe. God — The One who knows how many hairs are on your head, knows your thoughts, your dreams, your hopes, longs to walk with you through the good, the bad, and the ugly. God won't leave you or forsake you. He will be with you always.

Whatever happens in life, whatever you are going through, and whatever you face, remember that God loves you. He won't leave or forsake you.

Remember and always meditate on God's truth — You are loved, never alone, never forgotten, and forever in God's care.

Mining for Treasure

Take a moment to list some of the things that are happening in your life. Then beside each circumstance, situation, or difficulty, write "God loves me and is with me."

~ *From Screaming, to "Let's Go Again!"* ~

The other evening, we watched two videos made by a soft drink company with race driver, Jeff Gordon.

Jeff, disguised as an older gentleman, visited a car dealership and took an unsuspecting car salesman on the test drive of his life. You can watch the video (with over 44 million views) on YouTube.

The poor car salesman was terrified, horrified, and screamed during much of the wild, fast-speed "test" drive. By the time Jeff pulled back in the sales lot, the salesman jumped out of the car ready to call the police. But when Jeff identified himself, the man's face showed relief, then delight. And he immediately asked, "Want to do it again?"

Once the video went viral, several journalists claimed the video was a fake. The soft drink company and Jeff again teamed up. Disguised as a cab drive, Jeff took one of the unsuspecting automotive journalists who had questioned the authenticity of the original "Test Drive" on a hair-raising, crazy ride. The man screamed, kicked, and begged to get out, and yet when Jeff came to a stop and identified himself, the journalist wanted to go again.

The thing that struck me was, how many times do people (even Christians) beg, scream, curse, and demand to get out of difficult situations -- even though **God is in control**, even though The One who loves us best, who will never fail us or forsake us, is in control.

What if we truly realized this fact and enjoyed the ride?

What if we remembered (never forgot) that God is with us, and His power, wisdom, and strength are in the driving seat?

What if we joyfully buckled in knowing that each trial, each wild ride, results in more strength, power, and knowledge that God is in control, and our faith is growing stronger?

Let's do it again! Let's trust God to drive us safely home!

Mining for Treasure

Consider the following verses and underline the treasured truth to help you be ready always to go wherever the Lord leads.

"Consider it pure joy, my brothers and sisters, whenever you face trials of many kinds, because you know that the testing of your faith produces perseverance. Let perseverance finish its work so that you may be mature and complete, not lacking anything." ~ James 1:2-4 (NIV)

"Have I not commanded you? Be strong and courageous! Do not tremble or be dismayed, for the Lord your God is with you wherever you go." ~ Joshua 1:9 (NASB)

"So be truly glad. There is wonderful joy ahead, even though you must endure many trials for a little while. These trials will show that your faith is genuine. It is being tested as fire tests and purifies gold—though your faith is far more precious than mere gold. So, when your faith remains strong through many trials, it will bring you much praise and glory and honor on the day when Jesus Christ is revealed to the whole world." ~ 1 Peter 1:6-7 (NLT)

~ *Gifting Hope* ~

It's so easy to get depressed and distracted by the suffering in the world. So easy to wonder if there is any hope. Oh friends, there is always hope, because hope is Jesus! You are here "for such a time as this", you have been equipped to do whatever God calls you to accomplish. He will help you through whatever difficulties you face now and in the future.

Walk in His love and His truth, hold out open hands to the nail-scarred hands. Have your heart open to The One who made your heart. Love deep with The Love who loves deep. Share freely of the blessings, He has blessed you with. And watch in amazement as The God of the impossible makes all things possible!

Will you join me in helping?

So many organizations provide for those who are suffering, those who are persecuted, those who are hungry for God's word, please join me in helping. Join me in prayer. Join me in financial help. Even $5.00 can make the difference and give life to a hungry soul. Let's share freely, because our God has given us so very much.

Give the gift of hope, because we have been gifted eternal hope!

Mining for Treasure

Please consider the following verse and quote:

"Give, and it will be given to you. They will pour into your lap a good measure—pressed down, shaken together, and running over. For by your standard of measure it will be measured to you in return." ~ Luke 6:38 (NASB)

Holocaust survivor, Corrie Ten Boom wrote, "I have held many things in my hands, and I have lost them all; but whatever I have placed in God's hands, that I still possess."

What will you give God?

~ *Out of this world* ~

Christians live in the world, but we have been called out of the world. James warns us to be careful not to adjust God's moral code to fit the moral code of society. Do you not know that friendship with the world is hostility to God? (James 4:4)

Tweaking or altering God's commandments to fit "modern" times, or to help others feel more comfortable in their sinful lives, doesn't help them find saving grace.

Satan twists and manipulates God's word to make others fall and not find Christ. Manipulating God's word so someone may feel better, does not give a pathway to The Light, but leads to eternal darkness.

As Christians, true followers of Christ, those who obey Christ, we are here to point others to Christ. We are set apart for a purpose, and that purpose is a relationship with God above all other relationships.

Christianity isn't about making someone feel comfortable in their sin, but to help lead them to Christ. Jesus washes all sin clean and gives new hope, new life, and is The Way to eternal life.

Would you rather tell someone their choices are leading them down the wrong path, or pat them on the back and let them stay on the road leading to hell?

We don't need to make our world comfortable. We need to make the world aware of their need for a Savior.

Loving someone doesn't embrace their sin, true love makes sure our loved ones will be safe for eternity.

Loving someone is pointing them to Jesus. Jesus, who loved me enough to show me my sin and my need for His grace. Jesus, who came to rescue sinners. Jesus, whose love flows free to all who will come.

For those who are on the fence, for those who want to live your own life free from God's "restraints," please don't waste another moment. If you don't know Jesus as Lord and Savior of your life, if you only know His name, but don't follow Him and obey Him, please turn to Him. Please don't risk your life and your eternity. God's commands aren't to restrain you, but to free you.

For those who wear the title of Christian, wake up! Our world needs Jesus!

Be a light to the world, to lead the world to The Light!

Remember, "Let your light shine before others, that they may see your good deeds and glorify your Father in heaven." ~ Matthew 5:16 (NIV)

Jesus promises, "I am the light of the world. Whoever follows me will never walk in darkness but will have the light of life." ~ John 8:12 (NIV)

Mining for Treasure

Has God brought someone to mind who needs Jesus?

Please make sure your salvation is secure. Please make sure you tell them to stay in the light of Christ.

Don't waste a moment. Safety for eternity is at stake.

~ *Through the Door* ~

Our little dog is now eighty-four in dog years. He's getting a little cranky, can't go down the stairs anymore by himself, and has been getting up all hours of the night needing to go outside. His eyesight is dim, and he hesitates at the back door to make sure the screen door is open. He can't see the screen, so I usually tap a foot on the doorframe to show him it's safe to proceed.

The other night, I walked through the door to prove it was open, and he followed without hesitation.

How many times I've wanted to see God not just open the door but walk through so I had His footprints to follow.

And then I realized, Jesus is The Life, The Way, and The Door. So, when our life is filled with the life of Jesus, we are living in The Door and The Way.

Jesus is The Doorway to eternal life. So, when we have Jesus, we have the guidance needed, the wisdom needed, and as we follow Him, He leads us and reveals the way.

Join me in joyfully rejoicing that we can enter through The Door to always know The Way!

Jesus said, "I am the way, and the truth, and the life; no one comes to the Father but through Me.'" ~ John 14:6 (NASB)

"I am the door; if anyone enters through Me, he will be saved, and will go in and out and find pasture." ~ John 10:9 (NASB)

"But he who enters by the door is a shepherd of the sheep. To him the doorkeeper opens, and the sheep hear his voice, and he calls his own sheep by name and leads them out." ~ John 10:2-3 (NASB)

Mining for Treasure

Take some quiet time to become more aware of Jesus' presence in your life right now.

Where might He be leading you at this time?

What wisdom might He be speaking into your life in the midst of your current circumstances?

God has promised to provide His guidance to us. You can trust our Heavenly Father's promises! "Whether you turn to the right or to the left, your ears will hear a voice behind you, saying 'This is the way; walk in it.'" ~ Isaiah 30:21

~ *A Word to The Weary, To Those Trying to Live Out Their Callings* ~

There are so many working diligently for the Lord and not seeing the fruits of their labor. It. is. so. hard. to keep on keeping on when earthly blessings don't seem to be coming, and so very hard to focus on the eternal.

God takes the loaves and fishes of meager offerings and multiplies it to ripple out through His touch. Our God does amazing things when we offer ourselves back to Him.

Now you, yes you. You who are wondering if what you do is worthwhile. You, the one with long sleepless nights with baby in arms, the caretaker, the employee working fourteen-hour days, the blogger/writer who keeps writing, the unsung heroes without anyone to notice.

Please know you do make a difference! You are designed with a unique calling and purpose that no one else on this entire planet can accomplish. Many won't win public accolades or awards, we are all on different paths, we all have a calling, and seasons for those callings.

My sweet friend, Emily Wierenga gave me permission to share her quote with you. Other people, *"have their callings; you and I have ours. We are all a part of the Body of Christ. ... I just want to encourage you to lift your eyes to Jesus–to keep in mind that he lost everything when he came to the world, <u>so that others might gain eternity</u>. Our goal is to lead people to him, no matter the cost. ... The question to ask yourself is: Am I doing what God has called me to do with my life? And if you are, you have no worries because you are being obedient. But the thing is, we are to do what we've been called to do with joy and thanksgiving and a generous heart... these are hard things, and the enemy wants to steal our joy and he does this by* *planting seeds of jealousy and comparison. Keep your eyes fixed friend."*

Don't allow the enemy to steal your joy. Be obedient, follow God, stay on His path. You may not see financial gain or anything tangible in the earthly realm, but God is always working with, and for, His children. So be bold and brave. Behind the scenes of what you are doing, God is doing amazing things.

Keep doing what God has called you to do, keep fighting, and always remember even in the fight to rest in Him. Stay on His path, for God has you surrounded with His love and empowered by His strength. Remember the eternal blessings. Remember, never forget, your calling is about eternity.

Whatever you are facing, whatever your calling, whatever is going on in your life, please know you are not alone. God is with you, Jesus is in you, and your brothers and sisters are on the front lines with you. And when you are weary, rest in Jesus, and His power and strength will carry you through. Rest, weary friend, rest in Jesus.

"Come to me, all of you who are tired and have heavy loads, and I will give you rest. Accept my teachings and learn from me, because I am gentle and humble in spirit, and you will find rest for your lives. The burden that I ask you to accept is easy; the load I give you to carry is light. I will be with you always, even until the end of this age." ~ Matthew 11:28-30 (NCV), Matthew 28:20 (NCV)

Mining for Treasure

Jesus told us we will receive our reward in heaven. "Rejoice and be glad, because great is your reward in heaven..." ~ Matthew 5:12 (NIV) He reminds us that He came "that we may have life and have it abundantly." ~ John 10:10 (NASB)

Trust in the promise of our eternal reward, but don't miss the blessings and fullness of life that Jesus provides us with each day.

In what ways does your calling bless you each day?

How can you be a blessing to others in your work/vocation?

If you are a homemaker taking care of little ones, please remember that taking care of His children is one of our highest callings; for Jesus valued children greatly. Jesus said, "Let the little children come to me, and do not hinder them, for the kingdom of heaven belongs to such as these." ~ Matthew 19:14 (NIV)

~ Who Am I? ~

Do you ever wonder who you are? Perhaps it's just me, but even though I wear many hats, I wonder at times who I am.

This morning while I pondered that question, I felt the Lord's gentle question ... **"Does it matter who you are or <u>whose you are</u>?**

Oh my, Whose I am is the answer and solution to everything!

I belong to the great I AM who knows all, who loves with an unfailing love, who never leaves or forsakes, who has all wisdom, glory, honor, and power, and whose grace saves.

God is all we need, and all we need is found in God. I am His, that's who I am.

And that's who you are, who you can be – His! "My beloved is mine, and I am His." ~ Song of Solomon 2:16 (NASB)

Mining for Treasure

Does "Where you are" rather than "who you are" help you see yourself in God's sight rather than through the world's limited vision?

You belong to the great I AM who knows all, who loves with an unfailing love, who never leaves or forsakes, who has all wisdom, glory, honor, and power, and whose grace saves. God is all you need, and all you need is found in God. You are His, that's who you are!

~ *Hugged Tight* ~

Ever hugged someone, really needing that hug, and they didn't respond or pushed back way too soon?

God doesn't ever let go.

God never pushes you away because He is too busy.

He never pushes you away because He doesn't love you.

He never pushes you away because He doesn't want you.

God never pushes you away, because He does love you.

He never pushes you away, because He loves you now and forever.

God's hugs are soul-deep, soul-filling, and soul-satisfying.

Need a hug? God's arms are wide open and waiting just for you.

God is Love. And God's love, His hugs, hold tight forever and ever and ever.

Mining for Treasure

Close your eyes and imagine the warmth, security, and pure love God has for you. The wonderful thing is, you don't have to imagine what is real and true. God truly loves you!

~ Sick, Weak, and Feeble~

In preparation for a retreat, my friends and I spent months diving deep into the truths found in the book of James. While researching, we came upon some awesome realities in the verses below.

"Is anyone among you sick? Then he must call for the elders of the church and they are to pray over him, anointing him with oil in the name of the Lord; and the prayer offered in faith will restore the one who is sick, and the Lord will raise him up, and if he has committed sins, they will be forgiven him." ~ James 5:14-15 (NASB)

The original Greek is incredibly rich and in looking at the words used for *sick*, *restore/save*, and *raise*, we found wider applications than our limited English vocabulary.

1. sick - Lexicon: Strong's G770 – astheneō ἀσθενέω (to be weak, feeble, to be without strength, powerless, to be weak in means, needy, poor, diseased)

2. save - Lexicon :: Strong's G4982 – sōzō σῴζω [to make whole, be whole, heal, to save, keep safe and sound, to rescue from danger or destruction one (from injury or peril), to save a suffering one (from perishing), i.e. one suffering from disease, restore to health, to preserve one who is in danger of destruction, rescue, to save in the technical biblical sense, Negatively to deliver from the penalties of the Messianic judgment, to save from the evils which obstruct the reception of the Messianic]

3. sick - Lexicon: Strong's G2577 – kamnō κάμνω (to grow weary, be weary, to be sick, be wearied, faint)

4. raise - Lexicon: Strong's G1453 – egeirō ἐγείρω (to arouse, cause to rise, to arouse from sleep, to awake, to arouse from the sleep of death, to recall the dead to life, to cause to rise from a seat or bed etc., to raise up, produce, to cause to appear, bring before the public, stir up, against one, to raise up i.e. cause to be born of buildings, construct, erect, rise again, raise again)

Those times when you are sick, weak, and powerless, pray and call for others to pray for you. And those prayers will heal, save, restore, and make you whole. When you are weary, fainting, sick, the Lord will raise you up, arouse your soul, and bring you back to life.

God's word is applicable for *every* moment of our journey. Through the hard times, the good times, the really bad times, God's Word is available to restore and renew.

No matter how sick, weak, or feeble you may be, God's Word is soul-deep to cover every soul-deep need.

Mining for Treasure

Where does your soul need strength, healing, or awakening? You truly have a Great Physician who through His word will provide exactly what you need.

~ *Create* ~

Sunday morning church as we stood to sing, I noticed a drawing the little girl in front of us had made. A heart, and inside two figures, one bigger than the other, and over the picture she had told her teacher she loved her. The little girl's creation was a beautiful picture of love for her teacher. And my heart smiled as I realized within each of us is a desire, need, and passion to create.

Every day we have opportunities to create. We can create peace by turning to The One who is peace. We can create goodness by abiding in the goodness of God. As moms and dads, we can create a home with loving arms, not perfect, but loving arms that point to a perfect Savior.

We can create meals that feed the hungry (whether at home or beyond). We can create a smile and joy by being a blessing in words and deeds. We can write, call, email, Tweet, post, pin, and share photos that create points to ponder, encourage, and bless.

Enjoy the creativity of The Creator by allowing Him to fully create in you all that He has planned for you.

We are created by The Creator to create, especially to create room in our hearts for His love. "For we are His workmanship, created in Christ Jesus for good works, which God prepared beforehand so that we would walk in them." ~ Ephesians 2:10 (NASB)

Mining for Treasure

Watch for how you can create blessings for someone that will reflect God's love.

~ *No One Noticed* ~

Ever poured your heart out, said something, written something, made something, and no one noticed? And you waited, perhaps even tried again, and still no one noticed. And you wondered why you risked your heart and why you even tried.

The soul cries when no one notices.

And I wonder how does God feel? How does God feel when day after day He sends beauty, and blessings, and love, and pours out His heart, and no one notices?

God is searching for those who notice. God is watching for those He can strengthen and help. "The eyes of the LORD search the whole earth in order to strengthen those whose hearts are fully committed to him." ~ 2 Chronicles 16:9 (NLT)

God notices, He cares, He loves, He longs for those who will turn to Him, those who will seek His face and run to His loving heart.

God notices you. Will you notice Him?

Heavenly Father, please forgive me when I grieve You by not noticing all You do, and all the blessings You bring, and all that You are. Please give me eyes to see, ears to hear, and a heart wide open to You.

Thank You Father for You, for Your unfailing love, for Your forgiveness, mercy, and grace. Thank You Father for the amazing sunrises and sunsets You paint.

Thank You Father for the air to breathe, the life to live, and the joy You bring. Thank You, thank You, thank You! I love You!

Mining for Treasure

God always notices you through the eyes of His unfailing love.

Where and how can you recognize someone who may be unnoticed?

Your kindness, your acknowledgement of another person, will never go unnoticed by God.

~ *Beyond the Vortex* ~

Life can be a twirling vortex. The to-do list already has too many things to do and the list grows as unexpected expectations are added.

So how does one do, more than one can do? By keeping the focus on The One who can do all.

As an ice-skater keeps their focal-point on one thing as they twirl on the ice, we can focus on God as life spins around us.

Keep the focus beyond the vortex; stay safe in the eye of the storm with your eyes on The One who calms all storms.

Mining for Treasure

Where is the storm in your life?

Are you focused on your difficulty, or focused on The One who can calm your storm?

~ Joy for The Troubled Soul ~

My soul is troubled, desperate for God's intervention, and my prayer this morning just repeats, "Oh God how I need you, every hour I need you." I come to His throne with my requests, and my soul weeps and groans, and yet, and yet, there is a joy.

Joy is silent as though sitting quietly, watching, and waiting to see how I will respond and if I will fully trust God.

I ponder the verses to be sorrowful yet always rejoicing and to bring a sacrifice of praise and thanksgiving. I know that even when the soul is in sorrow, praise and thanksgiving can continue. Even when the soul is in agony, there is rejoicing because one day all that is wrong will be made right and all suffering will end.

Joy now wears a smile and moves closer.

Through tears I watch and wonder how to pull joy closer and if I even should. Perhaps in this moment of so needing God's breakthrough, answers, and wisdom, I should be more emotional and more distraught. Then I remember the verse about the Israelites how as they sang and praised, God set ambushes to defeat their enemies (2 Chronicles 20:22).

Joy nods and smiles.

Through eyes watery, I sing... "*I love you Lord, and I lift my voice, to worship you, oh my soul rejoice. Take joy my King in what You hear may it be a sweet, sweet sound in Your ear.*"

Tears fall as I bring my sacrifice of thanksgiving and praise, and joy wraps tender arms around my soul as I weep.

Gentle words soothe the soul with the knowledge that weeping may last through the night, but joy comes with the morning.

Joy comes, joy is here, even when sorrow remains.

Joy comes in knowing that the Savior has overcome.

Joy comes because one day all tears will be wiped away and all sorrow will cease.

I curl up and cry in the arms of joy.

Mining for Treasure

Is there a sorrow that has been brought to mind as you have been reading?

Can you envision Our Loving Savior beckoning you into His comforting presence?

What truths can He speak into your heart that can lead you to joy even in the midst of your sorrow?

What truth is spoken in these very words from the prophet Jeremiah? "Because of the Lord's great love, we are not consumed, for his compassions never fail. They are new every morning; great is your faithfulness." (Lamentations 3: 22-23 NIV).

King David reminds us to have our hope in the One Who Provides: "Guide me in your truth and teach me, for you are God My Savior and my hope is in you all day long" (Psalm 25:5 NIV).

~ *Give Yourself Grace* ~

Someone is hurting, agonizing over the past. The sin from yesterday weighs heavy and the memories torment. You've taken those sins, what you've done, and given them to the Lord. You've begged for forgiveness, and yet the past continues to haunt.

Please know that anything you have given to the Lord – those sins, that thing you did, the decision you made that claws at your soul – anything that you have truly brought to God for forgiveness and repented, those things are received and forgiven.

Those tormenting thoughts don't come from God. Because when sins are truly given to God for forgiveness, they are forgotten as far as the east is from the west, thrown into the deepest sea, and remembered no more. God won't and can't torment with something He no longer remembers.

There is no condemnation in Christ Jesus. We are washed clean in His grace, so please give yourself grace. Whatever the enemy is throwing up from your past, remember you are forgiven, and thank God for His grace. Forgive yourself and praise God for His forgiveness.

We've all sinned and fallen short of the glory of God. Every. Single. One. Of. Us. We are messy creatures and yet so very loved. You, my friend, are so very loved. Please, please, please accept God's forgiveness for yourself. Because when you refuse to forgive yourself, you are forgetting the gift God freely gives, the gift that Jesus died to give you the right to possess.

Please give yourself grace. "I have swept away your sins like a cloud. I have scattered your offenses like the morning mist. Oh, return to me, for I have paid the price to set you free." ~ Isaiah 44:22 (NLT)

Mining for Treasure

Satan has been referred to as the accuser of our brethren (Rev. 12:10) and the father of lies (John 8:44). He wants to accuse us and remind us of sins that have already been forgiven. The Holy Spirit may convict us but will lead us to His provision: Jesus!

Remember to agree with what God tells you in His Word rather than what the father of lies wants to tell you. God's provision of a Savior for our transgressions was promised even before He sent His One and Only Son to earth for us. "But He was wounded for our transgressions, He was bruised for our iniquities; The chastisement for our peace was upon Him, And by His stripes we are healed." ~ Isaiah 53:5 (NKJV)

Take some time to allow God's Word to wash over you and remember that our sovereign and powerful Savior not only forgives you, but He delights in you! "The Lord your God in your midst, The Mighty One, will save; He will rejoice over you with gladness, He will quiet you with His love, He will rejoice over you with singing." ~ Zephaniah 3:17 (NKJV)

~ *Desiring Increase* ~

Do you desire more? More that will lead to contentment, peace, and joy?

Will you join me in praying for increase?

Heavenly Father,
Increase my desire for You.
Increase my comprehension of how You are working.
Increase my passion for You.
Increase my capacity to memorize Your word.
Increase my love for You.
Increase my knowing of You.
Increase my thoughts of You.
Increase my voice to speak of Your wonderful truth, grace, and mercy.
Increase my vision to see Your vision.
Increase my hearing to hear You.
Increase Your truth in me, so that I may not be swayed or led astray by the lies of the enemy.
Increase my strength to be strong for You.
Increase my love for others.
Increase my faith.
Increase my ability to understand Your ways.
Increase my contentment by opening my eyes to see all You have provided.
Increase my peace by centering my mind on You.
Increase my joy by staying in Your presence.
Increase my heart to beat with Your love.
Increase You in me, so I will decrease.
Increase my view of You, because You are what brings contentment, peace, and joy.

Mining for Treasure

What do you feel is lacking in your life? What do you want to increase in your life? Ask God to reveal His truth in your situation and to show you what really needs to increase.

Consider the following verses on increase. Which one(s) speak most to you?

"May the Lord make your love increase and overflow for each other and for everyone else..." ~ 1 Thessalonians 3:12 (NIV)

"Now He who supplies seed to the sower and bread for food will supply and multiply your seed for sowing and increase the harvest of your righteousness." ~ 2 Corinthians 9:10 (NASB)

"He gives strength to the weary and increases the power of the weak." ~ Isaiah 40:29 (NIV)

"He must increase, but I must decrease." ~ John 3:30 (NASB)

"Now may our God and Father Himself and Jesus our Lord direct our way to you; and may the Lord cause you to increase and abound in love for one another, and for all people, just as we also do for you; so that He may establish your hearts without blame in holiness before our God and Father at the coming of our Lord Jesus with all His saints." ~ 1 Thessalonians 3:11-13 (NASB)

~ *Don't Wait!* ~

The other night I dreamt someone had planted an explosive device. I yelled for everyone to run, yet some fled, but others didn't. Some just stood and looked at the device. Then a second device arrived, and still people stood around discussing and analyzing them, but they didn't run to safety.

Life's time-frame does **not** have guarantees. Don't think you can put off or wait to make the decision to follow Christ on your death bed, or that you are more intelligent than someone who is "religious" and that you don't need Jesus. Or that you can analyze and discuss Jesus, but not run to His safety.

You can't wait. You have to know Jesus as Lord and Savior of your life.

If you don't have a relationship, if Jesus isn't who you follow and obey, you won't get into heaven. Jesus is The Life, The Way, and The Truth. Ignoring where you will spend eternity is just plain ignorant.

Don't take a risk on losing out on the most amazingly beautiful offer from Jesus for hope, forgiveness, restoration, relationship, peace, and eternal life.

The alternative is hell. **Don't wait!**

Mining for Treasure

If you haven't made this life altering decision yet, what is standing in your way?

Our society has a moral code with consequences for making bad choices (prison, fines, etc). Our Creator also has a moral standard with consequences. Fortunately, Jesus is our advocate and will stand beside us on judgment day: "if anybody does sin, we have an advocate with the

Father—Jesus Christ, the Righteous One." ~ 1 John 2:1 (NIV)

If you have chosen to have a relationship with Jesus, take time to thank Him for this eternal gift and reflect on how your life is different since you made this decision. And trust in the work that has already been done on your behalf and is offered to you as a free gift, simply because your Creator loves you! "Therefore, if anyone is in Christ, he is a new creation; old things have passed away; behold, all things have become new!" ~ 2 Corinthians 5:17 (NJKV)

If you don't have Jesus Christ as your Savior, don't wait!

~ *Sacrifice* ~

God sacrificed His Son for you. Jesus willingly stretched out His arms on the cross so that nothing would ever come between you and your Heavenly Father. He laid His life on the altar for you.

What do you need to lay on His altar? Has anything become more important than God and a relationship with Him? Many people would have an altar full of possessions they need to sacrifice. Others have a job, child, or spouse for which they had always hoped and dreamed. When God asks you to lay something on His altar, what He asks is to remove any and all obstacles that stand in the way of your blessings and treasures.

Picture yourself standing on a mountain, the scenery is beautiful. You acknowledge your sins, that Jesus is the Son of God, and is the only way to stand cleansed and Holy in front of a Holy God. The temperature is perfect; the sun shines down, the gentle breeze blows against your skin, and you raise your hands in praise. Right there in that place you give the Lord everything of you.

Whatever possession you have, whatever family member or person you love, you hand them to Him, laying it upon His altar. "Take them Lord, I trust you with it all."

Nothing in the world matters but Him. The power, the grace, the joy and the love infuse your body — never have you known such ecstasy. You realize there is nothing to fear living in His presence. The world can take it all because you have found everything in Him. You can have it you know; you don't have to climb a mountain; you can come to Him anywhere and anytime. Your soul has freedom no matter where you are.

Every step you take to Him, everything that you give to Him, everything and every person that you sacrifice to

Him will be replaced by a deeper understanding, deeper love, deeper contentment, and deeper joy. He never asks us to part with anything without replacing it with more than you can imagine. Surrender is not defeat; it is the beginning of a joyful eternal life.

"I pray that out of His glorious riches He may strengthen you with power through His Spirit in your inner being, so that Christ may dwell in your hearts through faith. And I pray that you, being rooted and established in love, may have power, together with all the saints, to grasp how wide and long and high and deep is the love of Christ, and to know this love that surpasses knowledge—that you may be filled to the measure of all the fullness of God." ~ Ephesians 3:16-19

Mining for Treasure

What do you need to sacrifice and surrender to God?

~ *Knock Sense into Us Lord* ~

Anytime we allow the enemy's lies to infiltrate our thinking and then continue to ponder on the lie more than God's truth, we sabotage ourselves.

Will we remember God's promises that all things will work for the good to those who love Him and are called according to His purpose?

Do we ask why God? Or will we remember that even in our finite understanding God is all powerful and still in control.

God's word is a shelter in the storm and a light for our path. The more we know God -- the more we ask – searching for His heart in the matter, the more we grow and are not blown in the wind by emotions, feelings, or circumstances.

What if we ask God to open our eyes and hearts to Him during our trials?

What if like Shadrach, Meshach, and Abednego, we walk in the fire with eyes wide open to see God in the fire.

What if we ask God to give us strength not only to get through, but to shine?

Knock sense into us, Lord. Open our squinty little eyes to see the grandness of You.

Knock sense into us, Lord. Remove the scales of earthly vision that block the vision of You.

Knock sense into us, Lord. Pry our gritty, little tight-fisted fingers off the things that we hold above holding You.

Knock Your sense into us Lord!

Mining for Treasure

Do you believe God can use both blessings and struggles to help you see His presence more clearly?

What struggles or "fires" has He used in your life?

What blessings has He used?

Is there anything that keeps you from seeing God as your shelter in the storm or a guiding light for your path? Spend some quiet time with your Creator and allow Him to speak His truth into you in all your circumstances. He is present, He is with you always and He will not forsake you.

"The Lord Himself goes before you and will be with you; He will never leave you nor forsake you. Do not be afraid; do not be discouraged." ~ Deuteronomy 31:8 (NIV)

~ *Satisfied with Thimbles?* ~

I wonder how often we strive for life's possessions, when in reality what the world offers is only a thimble full of temporary goods.

Don't be satisfied with thimbles.

Draw deep into the ocean of God's living water and receive heart treasures that last for eternity.

Which will you choose?

"Don't store up treasures here on earth, where moths eat them and rust destroys them, and where thieves break in and steal. Store your treasures in heaven, where moths and rust cannot destroy, and thieves do not break in and steal. Wherever your treasure is, there the desires of your heart will also be." ~ Matthew 6:19-21 (NLT)

Mining for Treasure

What possessions are important to you? Are they able to provide an eternal reward or simply a temporary fix?

What eternal rewards has our Father promised you?

Our Creator has blessed us with earthly beauty in nature; as well as minds and hands that make things for us to enjoy. But let us never give more attention or praise to that which is created over the One who is the ultimate Creator. God's gifts and blessings are beyond what eye has seen or mind can comprehend!

~ *Restless Heart* ~

My heart is restless,
longing,
searching ...
I know it's You I seek.
I know only You can fill.

Instead I look to those around me.
Seeking a touch only You can give.
Seeking the grace only You can impart.
Seeking the mercy only You can bestow.
Seeking a love only You can provide.

I remain hungry,
dry,
soul destitute...

Until I turn to You.

Resettle me Lord in the unsettled world in which I live.
Renew me each day, for every day with You begins with
new mercies.
Rest in a restless world is only possible with You.
Remind me to build up treasures in heaven.
Restore my passion for You.
Re-fire me Lord, flame me for You.

Take my restless heart and
rest it securely in the security of You.

Mining for Treasure

Is your soul restless? Are you looking to people, possessions, or the things of this world?

Read the verses below and allow your soul to rest in The One who loves you best.

"Come to Me, all you who labor and are heavy-laden and overburdened, and I will cause you to rest. I will ease and relieve and refresh your souls. Walk with me and work with me—watch how I do it. Learn the unforced rhythms of grace. I won't lay anything heavy or ill-fitting on you. Keep company with me and you'll learn to live freely and lightly." ~ Matthew 11:27-29 (AMP & MSG)

~ Scripture Sluicing ~

Sweet hubby and I traveled up one of the scenic byways and crossed a bridge to visit some hot springs. On the river, divers with dredges moved through the water. Their underwater vacuum sucked up streambed material.

Rocks, sand, gravel, silt, and other minerals passed through the hose, any gold remained trapped in a recovery system, and the rest washed back into the waterway.

Studying God's word is a treasure hunt. Yet I wonder how many times we reach for the Bible only to find nuggets that fit our purpose.

What are we missing by sweeping quickly through? Are the diamonds, rubies, and emeralds of God's truth passing by without notice?

Paul writes, "All Scripture is God-breathed and is useful for teaching, rebuking, correcting and training in righteousness." ~ 2 Timothy 3:16 (NIV)

Pick up your Bible, savor each useful word, don't miss even one letter of the treasures God has in store. There's gold, diamonds, rubies, emeralds, and valuable jewels in those precious pages!

"And if you look for it as for silver and search for it as for hidden treasure, then you will understand the fear of the LORD and find the knowledge of God. For the LORD gives wisdom, and from his mouth come knowledge and understanding." ~ Proverbs 2:4-6 (NIV)

"And the words of the Lord are flawless, like silver purified in a crucible, like gold refined seven times." ~ Psalm 12:6 (NIV)

Mining for Treasure

Who in your life might need to hear about God's treasures hidden in His Word?

Reflect on the rich storehouse of truth, comfort, peace, and joy our Great King of Kings has provided to us in His Word.

~ *Desperate* ~

There are times a desperate longing for human touch overwhelms the soul. Please don't yield to the enemy lies to settle for love that comes outside of God's perfect plan, because anything outside of God's will can never satisfy.

Pressing into God brings God's touch. And God's touch comes soul-deep to meet the soul's deepest most desperate longings. The deeper the dive, the deeper the treasures.

That desperate longing that tugs on your soul, that feels as though your soul might split wide open, is a call from the true love who loves deep, wide, high, and longs for your love.

When the soul is split, then God's liquid love can fill every atom, cell, and molecule of the souls longing, God's love comes and soothes the desperation with peace, joy, comfort, and love.

Desperate? Press in. Press up. Press into God's touch. Press into God's heart.

Mining for Treasure

Are you desperate for something? Take all your desperate emotions, desperate thoughts, and desperate longings to God in prayer.

"When I was desperate, I called out, and God got me out of a tight spot." ~ Psalm 34:6 (MSG)

~ Fearless ~

O to live fearless! Not locked in the fear of man but pressed in so deep to our loving Father's heart that tears can be wiped, sleeves rolled up in the muddy world battle, and yet not lose joy.

I want to live fearless, remembering I am invincible, because all my days are written in His book, and ***nobody*** can mess with my Heavenly Father's timetable.

Ah to live fearless, unhindered and loving deep. To fully die to self to fully live fearless in Christ.

I want that for me, and I want that for you. I want you to live fearless. To fully live the life God has granted you to live. To not miss a moment. To have open eyes, open ears, and an open heart to be all that God created you to be.

Live fearless. Don't let the self-doubt, or the doubts of others hold you back.

Live fearless. Don't allow the enemy to steal, kill, or destroy the abundant life that Jesus brings to the souls who come to Him.

Live fearless knowing that perfect love casts out fear, and you are safe forever in God's perfect love.

I want to live with abandon, be unbound, unhindered, and completely fearless.

Join me! Let's live fearless!

Mining for Treasure

What fears do you have today? Will you bring them before our Lord?

Remember that when you became a citizen of heaven you were equipped with the power of the Holy Spirit.

"For God has not given us a spirit of timidity, but of power and love and discipline." ~ 2 Timothy 1:7 (NASB)

"For I can do everything through Christ, who gives me strength." ~ Philippians 4:13 (NIV)

You are equipped in Christ to live fearless!

~ *Wave Watcher or Wave Walker?* ~

Our week was filled with calls from family members in need from hospitalizations, surgeries, and complications. Another call came from 5000 miles away from a loved one in pain and our hearts broke at not being able to help.

The phone rang again telling us of the hospitalization and complication for another loved one, and again thousands of miles separated each of us. Then a typhoon hit where our son was staying, and a nuclear reactor reported a melt-down.

We prayed, prepared to travel if needed, and prayed some more and peace came. Peace in the storms of life.

I contemplated the time Peter walked on water with Jesus. A storm was raging, but Peter walked on that wild sea. He walked in peace, until he took his eyes off Jesus.

Late at night the disciple's boat was buffeted by the waves. But then, shortly before dawn Jesus went out to them, walking on the lake.

When they saw him, they were terrified, thought He was a ghost, and cried out in fear. But Jesus immediately said to them: "Take courage! It is I. Do not be afraid." And then Peter said, "Lord, if it's you, tell me to come to you on the water." "Come," Jesus said. Then Peter got down out of the boat, walked on the water and came toward Jesus. But when Peter saw the wind, he was afraid and, beginning to sink, cried out, "Lord, save me!" Immediately Jesus reached out his hand and caught him. "You of little faith, why did you doubt?" And when they climbed into the boat, the wind died down. Then those who were in the boat worshiped him, saying, "Truly you are the Son of God." ~ Matthew 14:25-32

Peter walked on water by faith, but when he used his sight, he sank. So, let's remember...

When the storms come, walk by faith not by sight. ~ 2 Corinthians 5:7

When the storms come, take courage; don't be afraid, for Jesus is with you. ~ Matthew 14:27

When the storms come, keep your focus on Jesus and walk on the stormy sea. ~ Matthew 14:29-30

When the storms come, invite Jesus into your boat, and peace comes. ~ Matthew 14:32

When the storms come, God will still the storm to a whisper; the waves of the sea will be hushed. ~ Psalm 107:29

When the storms come, God is a defense for the helpless, a defense for the needy in distress, a refuge from the storm, a shade from the heat. ~ Isaiah 25:4

When the storms come, don't watch the waves; watch the calmer of the seas. ~ Mark 4:39

When the storms come, remember Jesus said "in Me you may have [perfect] peace and confidence. In the world you have tribulation and trials and distress and frustration; but be of good cheer [take courage; be confident, certain, undaunted]! For I have overcome the world. [I have deprived it of power to harm you and have conquered it for you.]" ~ John 16:33 (AMP)

When the storms come, God will keep in perfect peace all who trust in Him, all whose thoughts are fixed on Him. ~ Isaiah 26:3

When the storms come, remember "one final thing. Fix your thoughts on what is true, and honorable, and right, and pure, and lovely, and admirable. Think about things that are excellent and worthy of praise." ~ Philippians 4:8 (NLT)

We can't walk on water with our Savior if we are staring at the wind and waves. When the storms come, don't be a wind and wave watcher, be a wave walker with Jesus!

Mining for Treasure

Is life tossing you in a storm? Jesus said, "Come to me, all of you who are weary and carry heavy burdens, and I will give you rest." ~ Matthew 11:28 (NLT)

Jump out of the boat, Jesus is waiting to bring you rest in the midst of the stormy sea.

~ *To Hear and To See* ~

Is the focus on what was lost instead of seeing what God has allowed you to gain? There is danger in not being aware of how God is working in our lives, and in not seeing what God is doing in us and around us.

The Israelites "didn't see the miraculous signs and wonders He performed.... They didn't see what the Lord did..." ~ Deuteronomy 11:3-4 (NLT)

If we don't watch for God, we will miss the blessings of the moment and the courage and encouragement for the future.

Ears that are too plugged by the activities of the world, can't hear the gentle whisper of God's voice. "My people have not listened to me or even tried to hear." ~ Jeremiah 7:26: (NLT)

When difficulties come, are God's amazing triumphs forgotten?

Are you staring so long at the ashes and compost heap that you don't see what is blooming?

Is the focus on your own desires causing God's desires to be disregarded?

In the quest for the temporary, is the eternal missed?

Ann Voskamp writes of the hope we have in the riches of Christ. "There isn't a loss on earth that can ever rob us of the riches our Lord has saved us for in Him.

Oh Father, open my eyes to see above and beyond the temporary. Let me see how You have replaced what the enemy has stolen. Give me eyes to see flowers beyond the ash and compost heap. Give me eyes to look ahead and not behind. Give me eyes to look at You and not on me or my situation. Give me ears to always be attentive to Your call.

Please gift me Heavenly Father with eyes to see and ears to hear, listen, and understand.

"Ears to hear and eyes to see— both are gifts from the LORD." ~ Proverbs 20:12 (NLT)

"Anyone with ears to hear should listen and understand." ~ Revelation 13:9 (NLT).

Mining for Treasure

Make a conscious effort to watch and see how God has worked and is working in your life.

Make a conscious effort to listen closely for His voice.

Make a conscious effort to be aware of any desire that takes you away from desiring God.

Make a conscious effort to remember your loving God is ever-waiting for you to hear and see.

~ *The Grand Symphony* ~

Life really is a grand symphony. In the beginning the word spoke and life began. At earth's creation, the morning stars sang together, and all the sons of God shouted for joy. ~ Job 38:7

Throughout eternity the heavenly music plays as God creates and God calls. Sin's disharmony corrected when the Word became flesh, Jesus, offering the masterpiece of grace.

Those who will listen, whose ears are tuned to the heavenly music, find life eternal breathing in their soul.

The word, the music, brings life. Those who read God's word, spend time not only talking to Him, but listening, they are the ones who hear His melody that soothes, saves, and restores.

We all have our part in this symphony. Every one created unique, for unique purposes, and when we join in Christ's orchestra, we are given unique soul-music that calls, beckons, and draws others.

Regardless of your level of talent, regardless of what you think you have or don't have, when surrendered to the Master, harmonic beauty is formed.

And oh, how amazing the music. Nothing ordinary, for this music blasts away enemy strongholds, sings lullabies at night from Heaven's throne, sets captives free, and brings holy pauses that brings rest.

Keep your eyes on the director. Know the words and the notes that will guide.

You're needed. Only you can play your part.

The conductor waits. Nail-scarred hands poised with love.

Come to the Grand Symphony.

Come to Me, and I will give you rest. ~ Jesus

Mining for Treasure

During a symphony, each musician has a part to play. If the pianist preferred playing like a drummer, and the drummer decided to pound out his own beat, the result would not be harmonious. However, when every instrument plays their specific notes, beauty is made.

No matter how small your part, you are needed. Keep your eyes on The Conductor and allow Him to lead you into the beautiful melody of your life!

~ *Stumbling into Him* ~

During my long journey of chronic illness, I spent the day trying to prepare for an upcoming doctor's visit—making sure all the medications were documented and what had happened during the last years. The list was extensive. Discouragement set in as I pondered how the battle with Lyme Disease had been such a long and difficult journey.

However, the neatest thing happened. While I searched through e-mails to find notes on health, I also found page after page of documented times the Lord answered prayers (tumors that were benign, cysts and tumors that had disappeared).

I found abundant blessings of friendships that stood firm through illness, death of loved ones, trials, and heartaches. And I knew they were all treasures sent directly from God's throne–God hugs–amazing, incredible, loving touches of God's provision and protection.

The process to discover negative information actually caused me to find blessing after blessing as I stumbled into God's presence.

Thank You, Heavenly Father for providing for all our needs. Thank You for showing ways You love us. Open our eyes to see beyond our troubles, to see You in all things. Help me Father to always focus on You—on Your might, Your grace, Your mercy, and Your unending love.

I pray for all who read this that they will see You, Heavenly Father, working in their lives. Show them the touches of Your love. I ask these things in the precious Name of Your Son, Jesus Christ, who is our Savior, Amen

"Give thanks to the LORD, call on His name; make known among the nations what He has done. Sing to Him, sing praise to Him; tell of all His wonderful acts. Glory in His holy name; let the hearts of those who seek the LORD rejoice. Look to the LORD and His strength; seek His face always. Remember the wonders He has done, His miracles, and the judgments He pronounced." ~ Psalm 105:1-5 (NIV)

Mining for Treasure

Ask God to remind you of all the ways He has provided. Look back at earlier notes documenting God's provision, protection, and encouragement from others.

~ *Will You Lay It Down?* ~

Will you lay it down? The thing you love, the person you love, the house you love, the job you love, the possessions you love? Will you lay them on God's altar?

Will you trust God with your most valuable possession? Will you have faith that what He asks will be the best? Can you trust Him with your life and with your loves? Will you lay it down without seeing the end results?

God presses our hearts to go deeper into Him. To walk in His truth, even when He works in ways different than we can conceive. He beckons trust. Trust to move forward with Him and believe that His eternal rewards far outweigh worldly success.

For as we relinquish control, as we die to self, we gain wings to fly!

Will you lay it down?

"He who does not take his cross and follow after Me is not worthy of Me. He who has found his life will lose it, and he who has lost his life for My sake will find it. Store up for yourselves treasures in heaven, where neither moth nor rust destroys, and where thieves do not break in or steal; for where your treasure is, there your heart will be also. For what does it profit a man to gain the whole world, and forfeit his soul?" ~ Matthew 10:38-39, Matthew 6:20-21, Mark 8:36 (NASB)

Mining for Treasure

There are situations, or even people, that are simply out of our control, but they are not beyond God's reach.

What or whom is God asking you to trust Him with?

Can you trust that He really is Sovereign in ALL things?

Reflect on His love, faithfulness and concern for you today and forever.

"Lord Almighty, blessed is the one who trusts in you." ~ Psalm 84:12 (NIV)

"I waited patiently for the Lord; and he inclined to me and heard my cry." ~ Psalm 40:1 (NASB)

"But you, Lord, are a compassionate and gracious God, slow to anger, abounding in love and faithfulness." ~ Psalm 86:15 (NIV)

~ *Count It All Joy?* ~

"**Count** it all joy when you fall into various trials." ~ James 1:2 (KJV)...

"When troubles come your way, **consider** it an opportunity for great joy." ~ James 1:2 (NLT) ...

Count it all joy? Consider it joy? Really?

How does one count it all joy when loved ones die, health fades, bank accounts are empty, the past haunts, family members torment, and the enemy taunts.

How does one count or consider it all joy?

As I pondered the verse in James, I researched the words used by James in the Greek and also by using the Webster's 1828 Dictionary (see notes below). Count and consider are deep words filled with meaning and truth.

There is great authority when we take time to consider what God has done, for it leads our thinking on the right path, the true path of remembering and knowing God is in control and that all things will work for good for those who are called according to His purposes.

James isn't suggesting a flippant Pollyanna attitude when facing trials. I look back on my life at the trials I've come through – molestation, rape, being stalked, cancer, divorce, eight surgeries, chronic illness, and many others – and I can tell you with joy all that God has done in my life through those trials.

I can tell you with great joy how nothing has been wasted. God has redeemed, restored, and turned everything the enemy meant for evil into good things. By God's grace, I can count the amazing blessings that have come through those trials. God's abundant blessings ripple and ripple throughout eternity.

And I consider how God will use whatever comes next, because our God is a great God!

I can joyfully watch what God will do, trust that He will guide, and my faith will grow as I press deeper into Him. And He will be with me (and with you), He is already there, and He will be there for whatever is to come, whatever may happen, and whatever will happen.

Joy comes by focusing above the thorns of trials and suffering.

Joy comes when we count what God has done.

Joy comes when we remember that nothing is impossible for God and all things will be restored and redeemed in His loving hands.

God never wastes a moment of our time, or our pain, so count (and consider) it all joy!

Mining for Treasure

Will you join me in considering what God is doing in (and through) your trials?

Will you consider how the trials of your past have helped in your spiritual growth and the spiritual growth of others?

Will you count it all joy, because the joy of the Lord comes as we consider all God does and all He will do through the trials.

Will you please take the time to pray and write out the ways God has worked and is working in your life?

Reflect on the notes from Lexicon Strong's from the original Greek. The words are so rich and filled with joyful treasures!

Count – Lexicon: Strong's G2233 – hēgeomai ἡγέομαι
Transliteration — hēgeomai
Pronunciation — hā-ge'-o-mī (Key)

To lead, to go before, to be a leader, to rule, command, to have authority over, a prince, of regal power, governor, viceroy, chief, leading as respects influence, controlling in counsel, overseers or leaders of the churches, used of any kind of leader, chief, commander, the leader in speech, chief, spokesman, to consider, deem, account, think.

The KJV translates Strongs G2233 in the following manner: count (10x), think (4x), esteem (3x), have rule over (3x), be governor (2x), misc (6x).

Consider – Webster's 1828 Dictionary

To consider, to view attentively, to sit by; to sit. The literal sense is, to sit by or close, or to set the mind or the eye to; hence, to view or examine with attention.

1. To fix the mind on, with a view to a careful examination; to think on with care; to ponder; to study; to meditate on.

2. To view attentively; to observe and examine.

3. To attend to; to relieve.

4. To have regard to; to respect.

5. To take into view in examination, or into account in estimates.

6. In the imperative, consider is equivalent to, think with care, attend, examine the subject with a view to truth or the consequences of a measure. So, we use see, observe, think, attend.

7. To requite; to reward; particularly for gratuitous services.

CONSIDER, v.i. 1. To think seriously, maturely or carefully; to reflect.

2. To deliberate; to turn in the mind; as in the case of a single person; to deliberate or consult, as numbers; sometimes followed by of; as, I will consider your case, or of your case.

~ *Just One* ~

One matters
One sin caused condemnation
One life offers grace
One act of faith brings salvation
One comment
One blog
One letter
One email
One Tweet
One Facebook post
One phone call
One hug
One tender touch
One verse
One smile
One dollar
One can change a life

Be the one...

Mining for Treasure

What is one thing you can do today to be a blessing to God?

What is one thing you can do today to be a blessing to someone else?

~ *Do We Love Enough?* ~

Do we treat sin like an errant house pet? Is sin something we tolerate, or worse bathe, powder, and perfume to make appealing?

Do we love God enough to leave our sin behind?

Do we love enough to speak truth to others and to ourselves?

Do we love enough to tell people salvation comes from more than knowledge; that a true Christian life is a relationship with Christ?

Do we tell others about God's love?

Do we love enough to warn people that hell really exists, and they have a choice where they will spend eternity?

Do we love enough to tell others that Jesus is the way, the truth, and the life?

Do we love God enough that His love motivates us to love with His love?

Do we love enough?

"And you must love the Lord your God with all your heart, all your soul, all your mind, and all your strength. The second is equally important: Love your neighbor as yourself. No other commandment is greater than these." ~ Mark 12:30-31 (NLT)

"There is no greater love than to lay down one's life for one's friends." ~ John 15:13 (NLT)

Mining for Treasure

Heavenly Father, infuse Your love in me so that I may love with Your love. Help me to love You so completely that I leave sin behind and reach out to others. Help me to love You enough that I will speak Your truth with Your love.

~ *Who Is Your Help?* ~

When looking to others—to man's wealth and provision, jobs, the government, our family, friends, our acquaintances—instead of looking to God, there will always be disappointment, sometimes anger, and often heartsick and hopeless emotions and feelings. Perfection can never be found in man, and any help from man can never be perfect.

However, we have a perfect God.

God is with you, God's promises are for you, and God loves you. For every need, every trial, every heartache, every need, for guidance and wisdom, God is with you in every moment. He is your help.

Read through the verses below. They are promises from our loving God.

"Do not be afraid or discouraged, for the LORD will personally go ahead of you. He will be with you; he will neither fail you nor abandon you." ~ Deuteronomy 31:8 (NLT)

"Even if my father and mother abandon me, the LORD will hold me close." ~ Psalm 27:10 (NLT)

"I [the Lord] will instruct you and teach you in the way you should go; I will counsel you with My eye upon you." ~ Psalm 32:8 (AMP)

"Even strong young lions sometimes go hungry, but those who trust in the LORD will lack no good thing." ~ Psalm 34:10 (NLT)

"My flesh and my heart may fail, but God is the strength of my heart and my portion forever." ~ Psalm 73:26 (NASB)

"People who do what is right may have many problems, but the Lord will solve them all." ~ Psalm 34:19 (NCV)

"The Lord will protect them and spare their life and will bless them in the land. He will not let their enemies take them." ~ Psalm 41:2 (NCV)

"You only need to remain calm; the Lord will fight for you." ~ Exodus 14:14 (NCV)

"But I will call on God, and the LORD will rescue me." ~Psalm 55:16 (NLT)

"See, God will help me; the Lord will support me." ~ Psalm 54:4 (NCV)

"The Lord will give them strength when they are sick, and he will make them well again." ~ Psalm 41:3 (NCV)

"But the LORD will redeem those who serve him. No one who takes refuge in him will be condemned." ~ Psalm 34:22 (NLT)

"Yet the Lord will command His loving-kindness in the daytime, and in the night His song shall be with me, a prayer to the God of my life." ~ Psalm 42:8 (AMP)

"For the LORD God is our sun and our shield. He gives us grace and glory. The LORD will withhold no good thing from those who do what is right." ~ Psalm 84:11 (NLT)

"The Lord will accomplish what concerns me; Your lovingkindness, O Lord, is everlasting; do not forsake the works of Your hands. ~ Psalm 138:8 (NASB)

"I know and rest in confidence upon it that the Lord will maintain the cause of the afflicted and will secure justice for the poor and needy [of His believing children]." ~ Psalm 140:12 (AMP)

"Your kingdom will go on and on, and you will rule forever. The Lord will keep all his promises; he is loyal to all he has made." ~ Psalm 145:13 (NCV)

"Be still and know that I am God. I will be exalted among the nations; I will be exalted in the earth!" ~ Psalm 46:10 (NKJV)

"For I know the plans I have for you, declares the Lord, plans for welfare and not for calamity, to give you a future and a hope." ~ Jeremiah 29:11 (NASB)

"And my God will supply all your needs according to his riches in glory in Christ Jesus." ~ Philippians 4:19 (NASB)

"For <u>nothing</u> is impossible with God." ~ Luke 1:37 (NLT)

So, who is your help?

Mining for Treasure

What verses meant the most to you?
Which ones comfort you?
Would you be willing to write verses and keep a copy to memorize so you will always remember - God is your help?

~ *Ignite My Heart!* ~

I'm trying to process the most amazing thought based on a quote from A. W. Tozer. He used the line "liquid fire" in one of his devotions. And I've been thinking about how God melts stone hearts and they in a sense become liquid fire — lava – ignited with the love of God.

Lava can be extinguished with water. But liquid fire hearts that burn with Jesus cannot be quenched or put out because the source runs with living water and the fire is kindled by God.

Oh, my goodness, do you realize the power that is available to ignited hearts?

After two men encountered the resurrected Christ they said, "were not our hearts burning within us while He was speaking to us on the road, while He was explaining the Scriptures to us?'" ~ Luke 24:32 (NASB).

Jesus encounters always lead to changed hearts. And hearts that ignite with His passion change lives!

Mining for Treasure

Will you be willing to pray with me? Make my heart Father, living fire for You. Keep my heart ignited for You. Ignite me! Keep me burning with desire for Your truth and burning with Your truth. Help me to burn bright with Your loving Word to ignite other hearts to burn bright as liquid fire for You. Don't allow anything or anyone to quench the liquid fire that burns for You!

~ *Share the Love* ~

Christian friends let's remember we are here to promote Jesus, not ourselves. Pass on The Good News that promotes Christ. Share Christ's love with a world that needs His love.

There is such joy when we can shine the light on others who shine the light on Jesus. Because Christianity isn't about us, Christianity is about Christ!

As a Christian we are chosen to bear fruit, to tell others about the amazing blessing of God's grace, mercy, and salvation. And to allow God to use each of us in unique ways to touch lives for Him.

I don't write like other authors. Some of the authors I admire write like an eight-course meal filled with goodness as their pages flow with words that grip my heart and run my imagination wild with the love of Christ.

Years ago, the Lord gave me a visual for my blog based on Habakkuk 2:2, "Record the vision and inscribe it on tablets, that the one who reads it may run.'"

My writing is like a gas station; readers come to my blog or social sites, read, and go. I hope to bless them with quick nourishment that keeps them looking to the Lord, pondering His truths, and wanting more of Him. And I'm happy in my little gas station attendant hat because that's what He's called me to do.

So dear friends, let's keep shining the light of Christ in whatever means the Lord has called for our unique callings. And when one of our brothers or sisters has a worthy blog post, Tweet, card, letter, sermon, quote, or book, let's share the good news that shares The Good News of Christ!

Mining for Treasure

The Bible shares the true-life stories of those who walked before us, and because of their faith journeys we can learn and grow. You too have a story. You also read and encounter stories of others that uplift, encourage, and nourish your soul.

In what ways can you share the love with others? Tell those around you what God has done in your life. Share the testimonies and writings of others to encourage the body of Christ and help plant seeds so those who are lost may also find the love of Christ.

Share the love!

~ *The Puddles Beckon!* ~

O the joys found in God's truth! God's word is alive and active, brimming to the brim with living water.

Jesus tells us to become as little children, and I sit and smile as His living water puddles sparkle and beckon with His cleansing truth.

Children know the joy and abandon of play, of seizing the moment.

Jesus says that whoever believes in Him that out of their heart will flow rivers of living water (see John 7:38).

As a child of God, will you join me?

Let's splash and delight in the beauty of God's wonderful living-water truths!

Mining for Treasure

Jesus blesses us with living water flowing from Him to us, and through us. Let's splash His joy to a world thirsty for His joy!

~ *Vibration* ~

I hurried to prepare for Saturday prayer group and couldn't find my cell phone. The house was dark and quiet, the sun not even up on the horizon, the family slept, and I searched the few places the phone could have been. Using the landline, I called. Even though the cell was on silent, I hoped the vibration would be loud enough to hear.

Praying, and poised to listen; I strained to hear a faint noise. Sure enough, the muffled sound came, but I couldn't pinpoint the location. I crawled on the closet floor, opened cabinets, and looked high and low. Nope. Nothing. I searched and used a flashlight to shine in dark areas and still couldn't find it.

But then I patted my back-jean pocket, and there it was. Seriously? Oh, my goodness, how embarrassing. Now in my defense, I am partially deaf and my leg had been having weird vibrations before my knee surgery.

However, this experience has made me wonder how often do we miss the whispers of the Holy Spirit? Is God's word deafened because ears are tuned to the noise of the world? Are the vibrations of God's truth ignored because the world muffles God's truth?

Please don't miss God's gentle call. Please don't misplace the guidance of the Holy Spirit. Stay in God's word, read His word. Memorize scripture so that even in the darkness, even when life is muffled by the world, you can always find and hear the vibration of God's truth.

Mining for Treasure

Will you listen for the gentle vibration of God's call to your heart?

~ *Grace Sprinklers* ~

God blessed me with such a wonderful visual as I pondered how we are conduits of living water. Jesus is the living water, and His water is what gives life – new life. His living water refreshes for eternity.

And as a believer in Christ, His living water flows from Him to us, which flows to others to bring His new eternally refreshing life.

Goodness that makes us sprinklers! How fun to think of each of us watering a dry and thirsty world with the love of Christ.

Let's allow His grace to sprinkle and flow!

"For the Lamb in the center of the throne will be their shepherd and will guide them to springs of the water of life; and God will wipe every tear from their eyes." ~ Revelation 7:17 (NASB)

Mining for Treasure

Will you be a grace sprinkler to lead others to The One who provides living water?

~ Be In ~

In God's light, the true light is seen. ~ Psalm 36:9

In helping others, comes help. ~ Psalm 41:1-3

In tithing, comes blessing. ~ Malachi 3:7-13

In serving, honor is given. ~ John 12:26

In giving mercy, mercy is received. ~ Matthew 5:7

In fearing God above man, comes freedom from the fear of man. ~ Proverbs 29:25, Psalm 118:6

In humility, one is exalted. ~ James 4:10

In God's presence, joy is found. ~ Psalm 16:11

In Christ, eternal life is received. ~ Ephesians 2:10

Be In!

Mining for Treasure

Throughout scripture you can find other verses and truths that apply to being "in"? Will you take a few moments to look through the Psalms for more "in" truths? Mining for treasure is such an enjoyable, soul-filling time when you look for specifics and find God's truth. Be "in" by being in the Word!

~ Love's Best ~

Have you ever talked with someone and walked away troubled by the conversation? Or you say something to a friend or loved one, and from their reaction, realize they misinterpreted your meaning?

Since we don't read minds, effective communication can be difficult.

However, if we are in a love relationship, what we hear and what is heard, regardless of reaction or circumstance, is filtered through love.

Can you imagine the freedom we would have if we truly understood God's love?

God not only loves us, God is love. He is love that isn't just an emotion. **God. Is. Love.**

If we are God's, if we are in a love relationship with Him, anything that happens to us, regardless of the pain and suffering, we can be assured is filtered through His loving hands.

Paul, who endured many a trial and hardship, wrote "we know that God causes everything to work together for the good of those who love God and are called according to his purpose for them." ~ Romans 8:28 NLT

Because of that truth, we can live in freedom. We can drive God's love so deep into our hearts and souls that we're not buffeted by the worries of this world. We can live like little children excited to see what our Heavenly Father has in store for each day.

"So, we can say with confidence, 'The LORD is my helper, so I will have no fear. What can mere people do to me?' We can rejoice, too, when we run into problems and trials, for we know that they help us develop endurance. We can rejoice in our wonderful new relationship with God because our Lord Jesus Christ has made us friends of God. And we have received God's Spirit (not the world's spirit), so we can know the wonderful things God has freely given us. For the word of the LORD holds true, and **we can trust everything He does."** ~ Hebrews 13:6, Romans 5:3, Romans 5:11, 1 Corinthians 2:12, Psalm 33:4 (NLT)

Mining for Treasure

No matter how rich the human love, nothing and no one will love us as much and no one can show us more that we are loved than God. God's love is perfect love, love that is beyond the gentlest touch, the sweetest kiss, and the warmest embrace. His Love is faithful, compassionate, gracious, magnificent, infinite, overflowing, unfailing, and eternal love.

Would you be willing to take whatever you are facing, whatever is happening in your life, and filter it through God's love?

~ *Stop Running* ~

The world is so very busy. The minute the alarm clock beckons from bed, the race is on.

I wonder how often running is really necessary?

Is the pursuit of the world, and the things of the world, what has caused the rush?

What if we stopped running after the world and only pursued The One worthy of pursuit?

In pursuing God, there is no weariness or exhaustion, because He is rest, He is strength, He is peace in the storms and peace in the moment no matter how hurried the moments.

Stop running. Pursue only Jesus, for He is The Way, The Truth, and The Life to perfect peace and rest.

Mining for Treasure

Do you feel rushed and exhausted?

Would you be willing to look at how you spend your time each day?

Is there something that could be removed from your schedule?

Jesus offers rest no matter how busy your day. Ask for His guidance and wisdom for the use of the time He has given.

~ *True Identity* ~

Life is full of changes. Some days bring change filled with joy and hope. Other times we are met with situations that alter our world. Spouses, children, jobs, health, and a myriad of problems strip away our identities, and we are left floundering.

Yet there is one identity we can hold firm to the end – our identity in Christ.

In Christ we are a child of The King, daughters and sons of The Most High. Our stability is solid on The Solid Rock. We are unchanged within The Unchanging One.

Heavenly Father, thank You that whatever changes come into our lives, we know Your love never changes. Your mercies are new every morning and Your compassion never fails. Thank You Father that our identities remain unchanging in The Unchanging love of You.

Mining for Treasure

Do you struggle with your identity?
Do you wonder who you are?
Remember always that your true identity is found in Christ!

~ Scrubbing Shadows ~

The other day when the house was nice and quiet, I took the opportunity to clean the carpets with our handy-dandy carpet cleaner. In the guest bedroom I kept scrubbing one spot. Yet no matter how much I scrubbed; the stain remained.

Then I stepped back and opened the door a little wider. And that's when the stain magically disappeared. It wasn't a stain at all; it was a shadow from the doorknob.

Doesn't that remind you of the enemy? He taunts with shadows from the past, trying to keep people from healing or moving forward with God. But Satan's imprisonment is only a shadow in the light of God's truth.

Don't believe any lies from the enemy, and don't believe you can never be free. Jesus sets the prisoners free because He is the light, the truth, and the way.

Shine God's light and His Truth will set you free!

Mining for Treasure

Is there a dark shadow on your life?
Will you take this time to bring that to God?
Ask Him for His wisdom, guidance, healing, comfort, and truth. There is no darkness too dark, no shadow, that can keep God's light from shining.

~ *He Is There* ~

Small and large situations loom around the corner. As I pondered what is to come, and what may come, I realized a truth that caused all anxiety to fall away.

God is already there.

Whatever comes, God is already there. There is no need to worry, because God is already there. He knows what will happen, and He will already be there ready to take care of every need.

Whatever tomorrow holds, whatever you face, God is already there. He is The I AM. He is present yesterday, now, and the future.

Whatever you face, you are never alone. God is already there with the grace needed, with the comfort needed, with the healing needed, with the companionship needed, with any need, He is there.

God is with you, He will be with you, because He is already there. "I am with you all the days (perpetually, uniformly, and on every occasion), to the [very] close and consummation of the age." ~ Matthew 28:20 (AMP)

Mining for Treasure

God doesn't have to run to catch up to you, or gasp in surprise that something unexpected happened. For whatever may come, God is already there.

~ *Messed Up* ~

Satan, the evil one, is busy trying to make a mess of lives. And many times, he succeeds.

But we have a choice. We can sit and stew in the mess. Or we can remember and NEVER FORGET that God takes EVERYTHING the enemy meant for evil and turns it into good for those who love Him and are called according to His purpose. (see Romans 8:28)

Those messes the enemy makes? Let's make him pay!

Let's make the enemy pay by standing firm and trusting God.

Let's make the enemy pay by choosing to praise God.

Let's make the enemy pay by telling others about our wonderful God.

Let's make the enemy pay by believing God.

Let's make the enemy pay by never forgetting that God will never leave or forsake us.

Let's make the enemy pay by keeping our eyes firmly fixed on God's truth.

Let's make the enemy pay by keeping our feet firm on the foundation of God's love.

Because no matter how big the mess, God is BIGGER! And God's cleansing, healing, restoration and renewal lasts for eternity.

So, make the enemy pay right now by praising, believing, trusting, telling others about God, and standing firm on God's truth.

Mining for Treasure

Whatever has happened or is currently happening in your life, make the enemy pay by turning your focus on God and praising Him.

No matter how messed up things might seem, choose today to win by winning God's way!

~ *Don't Take the Risk* ~

Would you risk everything? There is no guarantee on the window of opportunity or time. There may not be a last-minute chance. Eternal risk is not a risk to take. There are limits that can go too far. An open, soft heart can close and harden. Ears become deaf. Eyes dim. Don't wait.

If you are living outside of God's grace, at some point you won't be able to get in. Don't risk rewriting God's laws for your situation. Don't risk allowing society or social groups to tell you what is right and acceptable in God's eyes.

Don't let anyone sway you away from the truth found in God's word. Don't take risks with your eternity. Don't take risks with anything or anyone that takes you away from God.

The road is narrow, and the door remains open only a short time. If you wait too long, refuse to come to God when you hear His voice, continue to live in sin, there will be a time when turning back isn't possible.

Don't risk eternity!

If you haven't given your heart to Jesus and made Him Lord and Savior of your life, please don't take a risk with your eternity!

Mining for Treasure

Please take a moment to read through the following verses. The Bible warns there is eternal risk for not accepting Jesus as Savior. Make sure you know who you know and that your eternity is secure.

"You can enter God's Kingdom only through the narrow gate. The highway to hell is broad, and its gate is wide for the many who choose that way. But the gateway to life is very narrow and the road is difficult, and only a few ever find it." ~ Matthew 7:13-14 (NLT)

Jesus said, "Not everyone who says to Me, 'Lord, Lord,' will enter the kingdom of heaven, but he who does the will of My Father who is in heaven will enter." ~ Matthew 7:21 (NASB)

"Jesus was teaching in every town and village as he traveled toward Jerusalem. Someone said to Jesus, 'Lord, will only a few people be saved?' Jesus said, 'Try hard to enter through the narrow door, because many people will try to enter there, but they will not be able. When the owner of the house gets up and closes the door, you can stand outside and knock on the door and say, 'Sir, open the door for us.' But he will answer, 'I don't know you or where you come from.' Then you will say, 'We ate and drank with you, and you taught in the streets of our town.' But he will say to you, 'I don't know you or where you come from. Go away from me, all you who do evil!'" ~ Luke 13:22-27 (NCV)

"The Son of Man will send out his angels, and they will weed out of his kingdom everything that causes sin and all who do evil. They will throw them into the blazing furnace, where there will be weeping and gnashing of teeth." ~ Matthew 13:41-42 (NIV)

"However, no one knows the day or hour when these things will happen, not even the angels in heaven or the Son himself. Only the Father knows." ~ Matthew 24:36 (NLT)

Speaking of the Antichrist, "This man will come to do the work of Satan with counterfeit power and signs and miracles. He will use every kind of evil deception to fool those on their way to destruction, because they refuse to love and accept the truth that would save them. So, God will cause them to be greatly deceived, and they will believe these lies. Then they will be condemned for enjoying evil rather than believing the truth." ~ 2 Thessalonians 2:9-12 (NLT)

Please make sure you do not risk waiting to take Jesus Christ on His offer of amazing grace and eternal life.

~ *Finding Joy* ~

I've been pondering, chewing, and digging to try and understand "the joy of the Lord." The more verses I read, study, and dissect; the more I find a common thread.

Joy is found by spending time with God, obeying Him, thanking Him, reading His word, praising (through word and song), and abiding and dwelling in His presence.

God promises when we draw near to Him, He will draw near to us, and when we seek Him with our hearts, we will find Him. God is The One who brings joy, and Jesus is the one who gives access to The Father. When Jesus is Lord of our lives, joy comes through His grace, mercy, and love. **Joy is Jesus**, and the joy He gives is the joy we receive when we come to Him.

God's joy is the perfect picture of a perfect, loving relationship. The love God gives is the love we all desire. God is The One who will cuddle next to us when we cuddle up to Him. God is The One who listens to our hearts. God is The One who won't ever misunderstand, but will know exactly what you mean, even when your words are jumbled, confused, a desperate whisper, or merely a groan.

Nehemiah 8:10 tells us that the joy of the Lord is our strength. **In God's joy strength is found**. One of the definitions in the 1828 Webster's Dictionary of "strengthen" is to animate. Animate is to make alive, to give spirit or vigor; to infuse courage, and joy. Oh, my do you see how joy returns and rebounds?

Joy is found in the strength, in the animation of making us alive in the presence of God. And in the presence of God we are alive, full, strengthened, animated, and joyful.

Replace the pursuit of joy with the pursuit of God. For in seeking God, we find Him, and in His presence is the fullness of joy!

Mining for Treasure

Joyful delight is found when we spend time with God and His word.

Please make time each day to pursue God, for in His presence you will find His joy.

~ *God's Truth for The Weary Soul* ~

When you walk through the fires of life, I will be with you.
I know the difficulties you face, and I will gently lead you and your young ones.
When you feel overwhelmed by the flood of activities, wants, and needs, I AM with you.
Even when you can't see or feel Me,
I will never leave you or forsake you.
I hear your cry for help, and I AM with you.
Don't worry, I AM here.
I hear your request for wisdom for you,
for your family, and for your job.
I know exactly what you need and how to guide you.
When you are thirsty and hungry for quiet and rest,
My living refreshing water flows freely, and
My peace is always available.
When your strength is small, My power is great.
When you feel inadequate,
you are always sufficient in Me.
When you are worried your mistakes are too large,
remember My grace is unlimited.
In the midst of unrest and unruliness, I AM peace.
In the midst of heartache and pain, I AM comfort.
In the midst of your daily journey, I AM with you.
In the midst of the unseen daily mundane chores,
I AM the God who sees you.
When life seems impossible to handle,
I AM the God of the impossible and
nothing is too hard for Me.
When the pantry is bare and the checkbook balance is negative, I AM the owner of the cattle on a thousand hills,
and I AM your provider.
Even when you feel trapped in your situation,

remember I AM your freedom.
When the nights are so very long, I AM with you, singing over you and quieting you with My love.
No matter how crazy the day, no matter how wild the situation, no matter how tired you are, I AM with you!

Truth in scripture is from, Isaiah 43:2, Isaiah 40:11, Deuteronomy 31:8, Isaiah 58:9, Isaiah 41:10, James 1:5, Psalm 139:15-16, Matthew 11:28, John 7:38, John 14:27, Psalm 147:5, 2 Corinthians 3:5, Hebrews 4:16, Ephesians 2:14, 2 Corinthians 1:3-5, Matthew 28:20, Genesis 16:13, Jeremiah 32:27, Jeremiah 32:17, Psalm 50:10, Philippians 4:19, 2 Corinthians 3:1, Zephaniah 3:17, Deuteronomy 31:6

Mining for Treasure

Take a moment to look back over the list. Where do you need to remember that God is ever-present in your situation?

God won't just be with you; He is always with you!

~ Jesus Joy ~

I've been pondering life's difficulties and the reality of living in a very hard and harsh world. And then I remembered, I'm not a savior, and neither are you. Jesus Christ is The Savior. He is The One who came to earth to save. He is The One who can mend broken hearts.

I'm so grateful for Jesus, so very grateful for a Savior, and so grateful that Jesus is joy.

Jesus is The One who heals all wounds. He is the restorer and redeemer. He is The One who tenderly tells us to cast our burdens on Him, not to worry, to trust Him, because He will make all things turn to good. ALL things. Not just some things, not just the easy stuff, but all things.

God knows what you are going through. He knows all things, and nothing surprises Him. And nothing that happens, no matter how rotten man's actions to man, no matter how hard the enemy attacks, is out of God's redeeming, restoring touch.

Whatever your needs, whatever is happening, His grace will be there for you. His grace is there for those in need. His presence is present to carry you through, to carry others through, and to right the wrongs.

Trust God. Trust Him even when you can't see the good. Trust Him even when you can't feel the joy. Trust, rest, take everything to Him — every concern, every terrible thing that has happened, every terrible thing that you have heard about — take it to The Savior. Leave every burden with Him.

Although there may not be joy in your circumstance, there is always joy in Jesus. In God's presence there is fullness of joy. If you have Jesus in your heart, you have joy!

Joyous blessings to you all!

Mining for Treasure

Joy is not the pursuit of happiness. Joy is Jesus, and therefore if you have Jesus, you have His joy available 24/7.

Galatians 5:22-23 lists the fruit of the Spirit which we are given when we give our lives to Christ. And within that fruit is joy. You don't have to muster up joy; it's available in spite of circumstances.

The early Christians faced horrific persecution and hardships, yet they had joy. They experienced joy, because they experienced Jesus.

Now once again, joyous blessings to you!

~ *Emotional Emotions* ~

Emotions are so, so, sooooo emotional. Ack! They drain us with despair, fear, discouragement, hopelessness, anxiety, worry, disappointment, insecurity, self-doubt, comparisons, unsettled emotions, and frustration. Emotions are intangible tangibles that tempt us to turn our focus off God to unsettle our faith and trust.

The enemy attempts to direct our emotions to blame our emotions on someone, something, the situation, ourselves, or God. Satan wants us to focus on emotions and use human strategies, time-frames, and human goals instead of seeking God's ways, trusting God's time-frame, and God's eternal goals.

Verse five in Psalm 23 says that God "prepares a table before me in the presence of my enemies." The Hebrew word for "prepare" also means to set in order.

So, remember that even when the enemy is buzzing around our heads like a swarm of gnats, God sets in order those wild and unruly emotions.

Mining for Treasure

Lord, You are bigger than any emotions. The reality of You is bigger than any feeling. Help me to take the focus off what I'm feeling and focus squarely on You! For You are the Unchanging One, The I AM who is present in the past, present, and future. You are The Life, The Truth, and The Way.

Your Truth is The Truth no matter how emotional the emotions of my emotions. Help me to take every thought captive and bring every emotion back under the truth of You and Your Word.

~ *False Interpreter* ~

After Nelson Mandela's service, authorities discovered the interpreter who had been signing for the deaf community was a fake. Nothing the man signed was accurate, yet somehow, he had been given that position.

We also need to be careful of the interpretation of others when it comes to God's word. Make sure, very, very sure, that who you listen to, and who you read, is accurately presenting God's word. Please know and read God's word for yourself.

There are many false teachers, many cults, and many so-called religions who twist and deceive and manipulate the truth for their own gain.

Please don't limit your knowledge based purely on the teaching of one man or one woman. Jesus warns us "Watch out for false prophets. They come to you in sheep's clothing, but inwardly they are ferocious wolves." ~ Matthew 7:15 (NIV).

Know God's word so you will have discernment to understand God's word. Read the Bible for yourself. Study the verses. Take time and make time to know for yourself what is found in the Bible, so you won't be led astray.

Mining for Treasure

Bible study is possible regardless of who you are and your education level. Libraries and online Bible versions and study tools are available for all. Be sure, very sure, you know who you are following and that their teaching is accurate.

~ *Enemy Maneuvers* ~

The enemy had been busy assaulting with subtle attacks. Thoughts would flit by, one-minute depressing, another questioning, accusations whispered, unrest caused restlessness, condemnation pointed, disturbance moaned, and each thought would come just long enough to create turmoil, but not enough to be identified.

And then it hit me as I sent an SOS prayer request to a friend, that perhaps the enemy was keeping me so preoccupied with me, that I was missing praying for my friends and family.

Ack, I had been out-flanked and out-maneuvered by the enemy!

Satan is out to steal, kill, and destroy. Steal peace, kill joy, and destroy every moment of the day. Thank the Lord that God is greater!

God. Is. GREATER!

Greater is He that is in us, than the enemy that is in the world. God is greater than any thought, person, or situation that comes our way.

Be aware the enemy is active, setting up ambushes, smoke signals, distracting, and beating the war drums, but remember our God is GREATER!

Resist the devil and he will flee; take those thoughts captive and stand firm on God's truth.

The enemy is out to mess with us, but don't let him get away with it! Use your sword of the Spirit and slash away those enemy attacks. Battle stations, friends! The enemy is active, but our God is GREATER!

And that SOS prayer request I had sent to my friend? I found out she had just returned from a funeral of a family friend.

The enemy was trying to keep me so preoccupied that I wouldn't notice when someone else was in need of prayer. But now I'm on duty and in the battle!

Mining for Treasure

We have an enemy who stays busy trying to distract us and make us ineffective for God's kingdom. Don't forget if you are in a battle, others are also battling.

Pray for your friends and family.
Pray for those who God brings to mind.
Your focused prayers matter for now and eternity!

~ *Twisted* ~

The enemy twists everything. Anything positive, he attempts to make us see as a negative.

Family, friends, church, houses, cars, any possession, any human, any moment, the past, present, or future, becomes twisted if the lies of the enemy are believed. Instead of rejoicing in what is given, the complaint is made at what is not received. Instead of living in the moment, the past is continually replayed, and the future becomes an object of worry.

God's truth is the proper perspective, the correct lens from which to view our life and the world, the reality behind the appearance.

Whatever has you twisted, take it to God and let His truth untwist the enemy's twisted lies.

Mining for Treasure

Do you feel like you are tied in knots? Take whatever is troubling you to God and ask for His perspective to untwist your troubles.

Heavenly Father, help me to see through Your eyes and have Your perspective. Thank You for Your word where I can find Your truth. Thank You that You are above all things, and nothing is impossible for You. Untwist the knotted mess the enemy has made with the straight truth in You!

~ *Don't Give Up!* ~

Moms don't give up. Keep loving your family. Keep praying. Cling to God. Don't give up. Share the Good News with a world that SO NEEDS GOOD NEWS!

Dads don't give up. Keep loving your family. Keep praying. Cling to God. Don't give up. Share the Good News with a world that SO NEEDS GOOD NEWS!

Women don't give up. Keep being the woman God has called you to be. Keep praying. Cling to God. Don't give up. Share the Good News with a world that SO NEEDS GOOD NEWS!

Men don't give up. Keep being the man God has called you to be. Keep praying. Cling to God. Don't give up. Share the Good News with a world that SO NEEDS GOOD NEWS!

Young people don't give up. Keep being the person God has called you to be. Keep praying. Cling to God. Don't give up. Share the Good News with a world that SO NEEDS GOOD NEWS!

Writers don't give up. Keep writing. Even when discouraged, even when the words are so hard to write, and the crowd doesn't seem to notice. Don't give up. Share the Good News with a world that SO NEEDS GOOD NEWS!

Musicians keep singing and/or playing. Don't give up. Let your notes fill ears that need the sweet sounds of the amazing truth of God. Share the Good News with a world that SO NEEDS GOOD NEWS!

Whatever your occupation, whatever your calling... DON'T GIVE UP! Share the Good News with a world that SO NEEDS GOOD NEWS!

Don't allow the enemy to steal your joy, kill your peace, or destroy how God wants to work in your life.

Don't give up. Share the Good News with a world that SO NEEDS GOOD NEWS!

Don't give up!

"So, let's not allow ourselves to get fatigued doing good. At the right time we will harvest a good crop if we don't give up or quit. Right now, therefore, every time we get the chance, let us work for the benefit of all, starting with the people closest to us in the community of faith." ~ Galatians 6:9 (MSG)

Mining for Treasure

Whatever your occupation or calling, don't give up. God is for you, with you, and will help you through.

The world needs to hear the good news and you are strategically placed to share THE GOOD NEWS of God's mercy, forgiveness, and love.

~ Break Me Out ~

Whether through joy or sorrow, there are times I feel my heart may burst. Sensations tug, pull, and threaten to drag me under the current. Part of me wants to run and hide and never fully embrace feelings that drive so close to the edge. Perhaps it's a fear of losing control or crying too hard or laughing too loud. Perhaps it's a fear of fully embracing joy because the joy might end. Or the opposite fear that a sorrow might not cease.

So, I cringe and put up defensive walls against the swelling emotions, not allowing the tears to fall or the abandonment of enjoyment. And then my soul aches for missing the moments.

Oh, Father God don't let me miss the moments! Don't let me shy away from pain or from bliss. Knock down any barrier that keeps me from experiencing fully the life You desire for me.

Break me free, Father! Let Your light envelop my heart to enlighten my soul. Break me out of me to live fully in Your love, trusting You in every situation. Break me out to fly free in You!

"For God, who said, 'Light shall shine out of darkness,' is the One who has shone in our hearts to give the Light of the knowledge of the glory of God in the face of Christ." ~ 2 Corinthians 4:6 (NASB)

Mining for Treasure

God longs for you to be free in every area of your life. Will you pray that His light will shine to expose and break away any barrier that blocks His love and keeps you from flying free?

~ Bee the Best ~

Goodness I was so out of rest. I wear many hats – wife, mom, blogger, author, speaker, radio host, friend, sister, semi-decent cook, semi-decent house-cleaner... And I started to worry and wonder where I should focus. I knew that God should be first, then family, then what should be next? How should life be prioritized?

I went to my Heavenly Father and He blessed me with a visual. I'm a bee. Yep, a bee.

My job is to bee available to Him. He created me, and He knows best. And when I stay in God's presence, seeking His guidance, He will help me be the best bee I can be! So, I'm sitting here with a smile on my bee face, beeing content.

While awaiting further orders, how about a fun game of the **ABC's of Christian Bees**. :)

Bee Aware of the enemy, but bee **A**nxious for nothing

Bee Blessings

Bee Content and **C**ourageous

Bee Devoted followers

Bee Effective Christians

Bee Fragrant spreaders of Christ's love

Bee Gracious

Bee Humble

Bee In Christ Jesus

Bee Joyful

Bee Kind

Bee Loving

Bee Meditative on God's Word

Bee Noble-minded

Bee Observant to follow God

Bee Patient

Bee Quick to listen

Bee Radiant with God's love

Bee Strong

Bee Tender-hearted

Bee United in Christ

Bee Victorious

Bee Wise

Bee Xtra special by being who God created you to be!

Bee Yielded to do God's will

Bee Zealous to spread The Good News!

Mining for Treasure

God's word is treasured nectar filled with nourishment and strength. "How sweet are your words to my taste, sweeter than honey to my mouth!" ~ Psalm 119:103 (NIV)

Bee ready at all times and to bee your best, spend time in the flowering truth of God's wonderful word.

~ *Personalizing Psalm 23* ~

A book I read suggested reading Psalm 23 then asking the Lord if He had anything for me personally in the verses. So, I read each verse, prayed, and contemplated what God wanted me to learn.

I've now done this twice, and each time the Psalm becomes more personal, more vibrant, and drives me closer to His heart.

Below are my notes. Would you be willing to also spend time with the Lord and make His word come alive in your heart?

The Lord is my shepherd.
Heavenly Father, thank You for Your guidance, protection and love.

I shall not want.
Thank You Father that You promise to provide. Help me to want only what You want me to want. Make me desire what You want me to desire.

He makes me lie down in green pastures.
I'm sorry Father when you have to make me rest. Help me to be completely willing to do Your will. Thank You that Your green pastures exist regardless of my situation or circumstance. Thank You for Your gentle touch that beckons me to lie down.

He leads me beside quiet waters.
Thank You Father, for the beauty of your quiet waters, what amazing beautiful visuals You have given me to enjoy. Thank You for Your calm, refreshing, Living Waters! Thank You that You lead, please help me to always follow You.

He restores my soul
O Thank You Father for Your restoration, soul-deep, overflowing, abundant life restoration!

He guides me in the paths of righteousness for His name's sake.
Father thank You for Your guidance. Thank You for Your paths. Thank You that I am Yours, and in Christ I am made righteous and bear Your great name.

Even though I walk through the valley of the shadow of death, I fear no evil for you are with me.
Thank You Father that You are with me during the hard, scary, dark shadows, and even when death's shadows fall, You are there.

Your rod and staff comfort me.
Thank You Father for your correction and for Your staff of gentle guidance that keeps me close to You.

You prepare a table before me in the presence of my enemies.
Thank You Father that even when I'm surrounded by enemies, Your banquet table is prepared and available for fellowship with You.

You have anointed my head with oil.
Thank You Father for Your anointing which makes prosperous, takes away ashes, and fattens with good tidings. This prayer is based on the original Hebrew definition of anoint using www.blueletterbible.org

My cup runs over.
Thank You Father for the saturation, overflowing love of Your presence.

Surely goodness and mercy will follow me all the days of my life.

Thank You Father that even with my sinful past, the trials, hardships, and heartache, Your goodness and mercy are directly behind me, covering, healing, and restoring in Your grace and love.

And I will dwell in the house of the Lord forever.

Praise You Father for the honor and privilege of being Yours and having the promise of dwelling in Your presence now and forever. Thank You, thank You, thank You, Father!

Mining for Treasure

Would you join me in the blessing of taking time to read the Psalm and pray over each line? Write your prayer of thanks to God as you read.

"The Lord is my shepherd; I shall not want. He makes me lie down in green pastures; He leads me beside quiet waters. He restores my soul; He guides me in the paths of righteousness for His name's sake. Even though I walk through the valley of the shadow of death, I fear no evil, for You are with me; Your rod and Your staff, they comfort me. You prepare a table before me in the presence of my enemies; You have anointed my head with oil; my cup overflows. Surely goodness and lovingkindness will follow me all the days of my life, and I will dwell in the house of the Lord forever." ~ Psalm 23 (NASB)

~ Morphing ~

A frightening, horrible visual came into my mind, but then God blessed me by morphing that negative image into a goofy cartoon character.

The enemy is always trying to mess with us, but we don't have to sit in his mess. God's power is available to transform minds as we take those thoughts captive.

Any thought, anything that we think about or meditate on, needs to be examined in the light of God's truth.

If the thought isn't pleasing to God, it doesn't belong, so throw it out! Take those thoughts captive (every thought captive) and obedient to Christ.

Transformation is available through Jesus – mind, body, heart, and soul. You don't have to conform to the pattern of this world (how the world thinks, what they do, how they act), because if Christ is in you, the freedom of Christ is in you!

Take those bad thoughts and evil visuals and expose them to God's light and the truth of His word. For in the power of God's Light, thoughts are taken captive, evil is overcome, and minds are transformed and renewed.

Remember, "Do not be conformed to this world, but be transformed by the renewing of your mind." ~ Romans 12:2 (NKJV)

Mining for Treasure

If you are dealing with negative images and thoughts, ask God to morph and transform them through the light of His love so that you may live in His freedom.

~ *Put Down the Idol and Run!* ~

Where do your thoughts reside?

Do you worry/ponder/stress/think about yourself, your family, your health (or lack thereof), your job (or lack thereof), the person who wronged you, friends or how little friends you have, possessions, etc. ...

Remember, who and what you think about the most becomes your idol.

Run from anything that comes between you and God.

Mining for Treasure

Would you be willing to join me in prayer?

Heavenly Father, I want You to be my one focus. Help me fix my thoughts on You and run from any thought, person, situation, or possession that keeps me from You. Help me to think foremost of You and on what is true, noble, right, pure, lovely, admirable, excellent, or praiseworthy. Help me to love and focus on You with all my heart, soul, strength, and mind. And may the words of my mouth and the meditation of my heart be pleasing in your sight, O LORD, my Rock and my Redeemer.

~ *Sharing Blessings* ~

I haven't traveled the world, haven't touched faces of the hurting and orphaned in foreign lands. However, I can touch hearts. We have children sponsored in India, Mexico, Rwanda, Kenya, and other areas around the world. And my heart beats with love for the little ones who my arms cannot hold. I don't have millions to send, but I can help change lives through prayer and through what we can share.

You too can change lives. Pray. If your heart is heavy or moved to take action, please take action. Share with others. Even if you don't have much, your little will be multiplied in God's economy in beautiful ways. Only one dollar can make a difference. Only one person can change many lives. Don't limit God by your limitations. Our little loaves and fish always become abundance in the hands of Jesus.

Will you share Christ with others? Are you sharing the blessings God has given you?

Are you sharing your testimony to show what God has done in your life? Share freely, friends. For when we share, we bless and receive abundant blessings. "Give, and it will be given to you. A good measure, pressed down, shaken together and running over, will be poured into your lap. For with the measure you use, it will be measured to you." ~ Luke 6:38 (NIV)

Mining for Treasure

Will you share your blessings?

~ *Yes, Lord!* ~

"Yes, LORD, walking in the way of Your laws, we wait for You; Your name and renown are the desire of our hearts."
~ Isaiah 26:8 (NIV)

Freeing the Israelites from hundreds of years of slavery, God led the Israelites from Egypt. God rescued them from the Egyptians without any fighting or effort on their part. He had parted the Red Sea, for guidance and to show He remained with them, He provided a cloud by day and a pillar of fire at night. He had provided food, water, and protection along their journey.

When the people arrived at the threshold of the Promised Land, twelve spies were sent in to scout out the territory. For forty days, the spies traveled the country and found beauty, a land so fertile it flowed with milk and honey.

However, when they returned to camp, ten of the twelve spies reported a few positives but their focus remained on the negatives.... 'We can't attack those people; they are stronger than we are.' And they spread among the Israelites a bad report about the land they had explored. They said, 'The land we explored devours those living in it. All the people we saw there are of great size.'"
~ Numbers 13:31-32 (NIV)

What happened to their view of God? The same God who had miraculously and abundantly provided, had told them to take the land. Only two men, Joshua and Caleb from the group of spies, were willing to believe what God promised.

The Israelites refused to move forward. Yet Joshua and Caleb "who had explored the land, tore their clothes. They said to all of the Israelites, 'The land we explored is very good. If the Lord is pleased with us, He will lead us into that land and give us that fertile land. Don't turn against the Lord! Don't be afraid of the people in that land! We will chew them up. They have no protection, but the Lord is with us. So, don't be afraid of them.'" ~ Numbers 14:6-9 (NCV)

Joshua and Caleb had seen God's power, they believed and knew God would provide and protect.

The Israelites response to Joshua and Caleb? They wanted to stone them!

Joshua and Caleb said "yes" while the nation of Israel said "no." The disobedience of the Israelites resulted in forty years of desert wanderings and the death of the entire adult population that said "no."

Although Joshua and Caleb were sidetracked by the decision of the faithless, God never forgot their "yes". God blessed Joshua and Caleb with youth and vitality during and after those years.

Please remember, although we live in a faithless world, and many will say no to the Lord, we must be willing to step out in faith and obedience to believe and follow Gods leading.

For in following and obeying, we find the blessings of God for now and forever. "Whoever has my commands and obeys them, he is the one who loves Me. He who loves Me will be loved by my Father, and I too will love him and show myself to him." ~ John 14:21 (NIV)

Mining for Treasure

Will you say "yes" to God?

~ *Stuck* ~

I don't know about you, but some days I'm encumbered by "stuff." I get tangled and trapped in worries. Or my ideas and thoughts keep me from seeing and believing God's ideas and thoughts. And then my busyness results in accomplishing nothingness. I'm stuck.

I might as well be stuck to the ceiling with my arms dangling.

Paul writes in 1 Corinthians 9: 24, don't you know that in a race all runners run, but only one wins the prize. So, run to win the prize!

I know others have gone before us on the Christian trail. I love the translation from The Message version of Hebrews 12:1-3, "Do you see what this means—all these pioneers who blazed the way, all these veterans cheering us on? It means we'd better get on with it. Strip down, start running—and never quit! No extra spiritual fat, no parasitic sins. Keep your eyes on Jesus, who both began and finished this race we're in. Study how he did it. Because he never lost sight of where he was headed—that exhilarating finish in and with God—he could put up with anything along the way: Cross, shame, whatever. And now he's there, in the place of honor, right alongside God. When you find yourselves flagging in your faith, go over that story again, item by item, that long litany of hostility he plowed through. That will shoot adrenaline into your souls!"

Hmmm... Anyone want to buy a very used Velcro suit?

Mining for Treasure

Ask God to reveal any area in your life that has caused you to be stuck outside of His will.

Ask God to reveal any area in your life that is causing you to be stuck in running the race He has for you.

Heavenly Father, help me to keep my mind focused on You and my feet running to You.

~ Wealth Perspective ~

At birth, I arrived with nothing — no clothes, no belongings, and no speech other than a cry. Based on what I had when I arrived, much has been given.

No matter how little I posses, my riches are beyond measure. And when death comes, I can take nothing but the one thing that matters the most—an eternal relationship with Jesus Christ, my Savior.

Nothing is greater than knowing Christ Jesus as Lord, because everything else perishes, spoils or fades. So, don't put your hope in wealth, which is so uncertain, put your hope in God who richly provides us everything for our enjoyment. For an inheritance in Christ results in incorruptible eternal riches. ~ 1 Timothy 6:17-18, John 3:16, Philippians 3:8, John 3:16, 1 Peter 1:4

Are you eternally rich?

Mining for Treasure

I love this quote by Charles Spurgeon... "The whole of Christ, in his adorable character as the Son of God, is by himself made over to us most richly to enjoy. His wisdom is our direction, his knowledge our instruction, his power our protection, his justice our surety, his love our comfort, his mercy our solace, and his immutability our trust."

Regardless of your earthly status, credit report, clothing, dwelling, or job, you are rich in Christ!

~ *For You, Friend* ~

For my friends alone with children ~ God is a Father to the fatherless. ~ Psalm 68:5

For my widow friends ~ God is a defender and protector of the widows. Psalm 68:5

For my single friends ~ God is your husband and your Redeemer. ~ Isaiah 54:5

For those with young children ~ God tends his flock like a shepherd: He gathers the lambs in his arms and carries them close to his heart; he gently leads those that have young. ~ Isaiah 40:11

For those wondering which direction to take ~ God will instruct you and teach you in the way you should go; He will counsel you with His loving eye on you. ~ Psalm 32:8

For those who have been gossiped about or slandered ~ No weapon formed against you will prosper; and every tongue that accuses you in judgment you will condemn. This is the heritage of the servants of the LORD, and their vindication is from God. ~ Isaiah 54:17

For the workers ~ Work willingly at whatever you do, as though you were working for the Lord rather than for people. Do everything without grumbling or arguing. Stand firm. Let nothing move you. Always give yourselves fully to the work of the Lord, because your labor in the Lord is not in vain. ~ Colossians 3:23, Philippians 2:14, 1 Corinthians 15:58

For my friends, please know Christ as Savior and Lord of your life, for when you do, you are blessed with the ultimate friendship.

For those in Christ, remember the words of Jesus... "You are My friends if you do what I command you. No longer do I call you slaves, for the slave does not know what his master is doing; but I have called you friends, for all things that I have heard from My Father I have made known to you. You did not choose Me but I chose you and appointed you that you would go and bear fruit, and that your fruit would remain, so that whatever you ask of the Father in My name He may give to you." ~ John 15:14-16 (NASB)

Mining for Treasure

The beauty of a friendship with Christ is that you are called His friend. And in that friendship comes amazing blessings of His gentle care regardless of your situation or circumstance.

Take comfort, for your Friend is always with you for now and eternity.

~ *Don't Miss the Love* ~

Growing up in the church with Godly parents, God was always part of our lives. When I reached adulthood, I believed I was part of God's plan, and I would be used by Him. At one juncture, I tried to start a neighborhood Bible study. I had so much I had learned and so much I could share.

The study? It was a disaster. I was too focused on me and what I could do and missed sharing God's love.

No one needs to know what I think or what I know -- they need and want to know what God says, who God is, what God knows and how much He loves each one of us. That is the beauty of Christianity -- we do not need to have all the answers, we can point others to The One who does!

Love attracts and does not repel. Love melts away the bondage of sin. Love paves the way home for the lost. When we share the love of Christ, others are drawn to the love of Christ.

"A new command I give you: Love one another. As I have loved you, so you must love one another. By this all men will know that you are my disciples, if you love one another." ~ John 13:34-35

Mining for Treasure

What are some ways you can share God's love with others?

~ Hope for The Hurting ~

There are so many hurting people, so many lonely hearts, so much violence, trauma, and heartaches. Reality can be overwhelming. We can't fix the world, but we can rest in The One who can.

God promises ... "I will search for the lost and bring back the strays. I will bind up the injured and strengthen the weak..." Ezekiel 34:16 (NIV)

He delivers... "The angel of the Lord camps around those who fear God, and he saves them." ~ Psalm 34:7 (NCV).

"The Lord helps them, rescuing them from the wicked. He saves them, and they find shelter in him." ~ Psalm 37:40 (NLT)

"He will fulfill the desire of those who fear Him; He will also hear their cry and will save them." ~ Psalm 145:19 (NASB)

He watches and listens... "Morning, noon, and night I cry out in my distress, and the Lord hears my voice." ~ Psalm 55:17 (NLT).

"The eyes of the Lord are on the righteous, and His ears are open to their cry." ~ Psalm 34:15 (NKJV).

"I cried to the Lord with my voice, and He heard me from His holy hill." ~ Psalm 3:4 (NKJV).

He heals.... "He heals the brokenhearted and binds up their wounds" ~ Psalm 147:3 (NASB)

"Praise the Lord, my soul, and forget not all his benefits—who forgives all your sins and heals all your diseases," ~ Psalm 103:2-3 (NIV)

He is our refuge.... "He who dwells in the shelter of the Most High will rest in the shadow of the Almighty." ~ Psalm 91:1 (NASB)

"He will cover you with his feathers. He will shelter you with his wings. His faithful promises are your armor and protection." ~ Psalm 91:4 (NLT)

"The Lord also will be a refuge for the oppressed, a refuge in times of trouble." ~ Psalm 9:9 (NKJV)

He is our rest.... "Then Jesus said, 'Come to me, all of you who are weary and carry heavy burdens, and I will give you rest. Take my yoke upon you. Let me teach you, because I am humble and gentle at heart, and you will find rest for your souls. For my yoke is easy to bear, and the burden I give you is light." ~ Matthew 11:28-30 (NLT)

"My soul finds rest in God alone; my salvation comes from Him" (Psalm 62:1).

He is our victor... "These things I have spoken to you, so that in Me you may have peace. In the world you have tribulation but take courage; I have overcome the world." ~ John 16:33 (NASB)

God loves you. He won't ever leave or forsake you. His power is greater than any need. His love is more tender than any human love. God is with you every step of the way, every moment, and every breath. You are never alone.

"He will wipe away every tear from their eyes; and there will no longer be any death; there will no longer be any mourning, or crying, or pain; the first things have passed away. And He who sits on the throne said, 'Behold, I am making all things new." ~ Revelation 21:4-5 (NASB)

Mining for Treasure

Allow God's truth to provide hope and comfort for your hurting soul.

God is your deliverer, watching and listening, healing, allowing you refuge, rest, and victory.

~ *A Prayer for the Hurting* ~

Heavenly Father, we bring our prayer before Your loving throne.

For those who are lonely or have lost loved ones, please magnify Your presence and comfort.

For those whose finances are lacking, please multiply the loaves and fishes to meet each need.

For those who feel surrounded by the enemy, please open their eyes to see Your angelic army surrounding them.

For those who are groping in the darkness, shine Your light of truth and mercy.

For those who are homeless, thank You that they can dwell forever in Your presence and have a wonderful eternal home with You.

For those who are afraid, remind them of Your might and authority.

For those who are in difficult situations, shelter them in the shadow of Your powerful wings.

Wrap them tenderly in Your love Father. Hold them close as You wipe every precious tear. Bless them Father to feel You in a new, real, and vibrant way. Place in their hearts the joy of You.

Mining for Treasure

Which truth is dearest to your heart? Take the time to copy the verses to tape on your mirror in the morning, at your desk at work, or in your purse or wallet.

~ *Beyond Head-knowledge* ~

Make sure your faith in Jesus is more than head-knowledge. Even the demons know that Jesus is the Son of God.

True Christianity is beyond head-knowledge. "You say you have faith, for you believe that there is one God. Good for you! Even the demons believe this, and they tremble in terror." ~ James 2:19 (NLT)

True Christianity is beyond knowing scripture, attending church, and quoting Bible verses. "Suddenly, a man in the synagogue who was possessed by an evil spirit began shouting, 'Why are you interfering with us, Jesus of Nazareth? Have you come to destroy us? I know who you are–the Holy One of God!'" ~ Mark 1:24 NLT (Did you notice the man was in the synagogue? Not everyone who attends church is a true Christian.)

TRUE Christianity is knowing Jesus Christ as Savior and making Him Lord of your life.

Saving-faith is heart-deep, following, and obeying Christ.

Mining for Treasure

Will you go beyond head knowledge, to make sure your faith is heart-deep? Because God "desires all men to be saved and to come to the knowledge of the truth." ~ 1 Timothy 2:4 (NASB)

"If you confess with your mouth Jesus as Lord, and believe in your heart that God raised Him from the dead, you will be saved" ~ Romans 10:9 (NASB)

~ *You have today.* ~

Regardless of what happened in the past, what may come in the future, you have today. Don't waste a moment. Don't forget that God loves you. Time is short. The time is now. If you haven't asked Jesus into your life and made Him the Lord of your life, the time is now.

Hope, peace, joy, soul-deep-healing, comes through Jesus Christ. Jesus is the way, the truth, and the life. Life that leads to life. Jesus gave His life, to give you new life.

You have today.

Please don't waste a moment. The time is now. The arms of Jesus are open wide to gift you with eternal life.

God loved the world so much that He gave His only Son, and those who believe in Him, (in Jesus Christ) will have eternal life. God didn't send Jesus to condemn the world, but to save the world through Him. Because the wages of sin is death, God gave the free gift of eternal life through Jesus. And everyone who calls on the name of Jesus will be saved (John 3:16-17, Romans 6:23, Romans 10:13).

Don't miss God's ever-present gift for every day — Jesus. Don't miss the blessings of living every day (every today) with Jesus.

Mining for Treasure

If you haven't given your heart to Jesus, today would be a great day to make that decision! If you have given your heart to Jesus, take time to tell someone they too can make that decision today.

~ *Timeless* ~

The clouds blow by, ever-changing-moving, and so is time, ever-moving. Even on days that seem so long, so unchanging, and there seems to be no movement, remember you are here by divine appointment.

You are here for such a time as this. Whatever you have been called to do – at your job, at home, as a student, as a caregiver, wherever you work or live – do all for the glory of God.

Time is timeless; don't miss the time of now.

"The Lord keeps watch over you as you come and go, both now and forever." ~ Psalm 121:8 (NLT)

Mining for Treasure

Will you spend time in the proper ways so that time may not be wasted?
Will you spend time so that time is well spent?
Will you spend time with The One who made time?

~ Seeking God ~

Relationships are two-sided. God tells us to seek Him with all our hearts and we will find Him. Daniel's prayer in Daniel 9 is humble, repentant, and God honoring.

Daniel prays, repents for the people, beseeches God to hear and see what has happened. His prayer ends... "for we are not presenting our supplications before You on account of any merits of our own, but on account of Your great compassion. O Lord, hear! O Lord, forgive! O Lord, listen and take action! For Your own sake, O my God, do not delay, because Your city and Your people are called by Your name." ~ Daniel 9:17-19 (NASB)

Daniel walked the walk and talked the talk. And because of his God-honoring relationship with God, He was considered "highly esteemed" and "dearly or greatly beloved." Daniel loved God and sought His presence in every decision and every hardship. Daniel received honor from God because he honored God.

We can long for the title of "greatly loved by God" but time must be spent with God and His word. Seeking God's heart in all things and loving Him with every fiber of our being brings amazing, sweet fellowship. There is no better use of our life and our time.

Mining for Treasure

Will you be one who loves, honors, and seeks after God?

~ *Wasting, Wishing, Missing* ~

Winter in Idaho should mean snow. Here in the high desert country, snow melt is what provides our area with water in the spring and summer months.

Christmas week, our temperature almost reached sixty degrees, and I longed for the beauty of snow-covered mountains. I must admit I whined, prayed, and reminded God of the importance of a thick white blanket for our peaks. Then in my soul I heard the small voice reminding me not to whine and waste God's daily gifts. Ouch.

How many of God's blessings do we miss when we wish things were different?

How many days and moments are wasted looking for things to be the way we think they should be?

How often do we focus so intently on what we want, that we miss what God has already given?

What if we truly lived with the faith of a child knowing our Heavenly Father will provide for every need?

What if we truly trusted God?

P.S. A few days later, the snow arrived. :)

Mining for Treasure

Will you join me in prayer? Heavenly Father, please forgive me when I waste, miss, and whine away the blessings You freely give. Help me to focus on You instead of how I think things should be. Help me to let go and let You be God.

Thank You Father, that when You ask us to surrender to Your sovereignty it is for us to walk in freedom!

Oh, what joy when I submit to You! Thank You, Father. Thank You!

~ *Did You See?* ~

Did you see...? Have you heard ...? Did you know...? Do you remember that bad thing ...?

The enemy constantly clamors for our attention on anything and everything negative. Satan is out to steal, kill, and destroy – steal joy, kill our passion for Christ, destroy a positive outlook. It's so easy to ponder, wonder, agonize, and try to understand the terrible things that happen in this world.

Don't let the enemy win!

Jesus reminds us there will be trouble and tribulation, but not to worry or be anxious, because He has overcome the world.

Paul reminds us to fix our thoughts on what is true, honorable, right, pure, lovely, admirable, and to think about things that are excellent and worthy of praise. Be anxious for nothing, but in everything by prayer and supplication with thanksgiving let your requests be made known to God. And the peace of God, which surpasses all comprehension, will guard your hearts and your minds in Christ Jesus.

When those negative thoughts come calling, take them captive!

Let the meditations of your mouth and your heart be pleasing to God. And in return, your focus refocuses on the power, might, strength, loving-kindness, and compassion of our God; the God who defeats all foes and turns mourning into joy.

So next time the enemy beckons for you to see the bad stuff, to focus on the negative, respond with praise and thanksgiving for who our God is, for what He has done, and for His eternal love, grace, and mercy.

~ Compiled from John 10:10, John 16:33, Matthew 6:34, Philippians 4:8, Philippians 4:6-7, 2 Corinthians 10:5, Psalm 19:14, Ephesians 6:10, Psalm 145, Revelation 21:4

Mining for Treasure

Will you pray with me?

Heavenly Father, open my eyes to see how You are working in my life and in the world. Open my eyes to see the joy beyond the thorns of hardships, trials, and suffering. Open my eyes to see joy above the rocky roads of uncertainty and worries. Open my eyes Father to see You and Your joy!

"Those who look to Him for help will be radiant with joy; no shadow of shame will darken their faces." ~ Psalm 34:5 (NLT)

~ *Remember* ~

I woke in the middle of the night with the word, "Remember" echoing in my thoughts.

Pondering what God wanted me to remember, I opened my Bible to search for scripture. And there in the margin of my Bible was a note from March 2009 titled, "Boise Promise."

In April of 2009 we moved from Texas to Boise, Idaho. And the verse highlighted is "He is your praise and He is your God, who has done these great and awesome things for you which your eyes have seen." ~ Deuteronomy 10:21 (NASB)

And the memories returned as I remembered the great and awesome things I have seen. Since March of 2009 I remember the things God has done, the awesome and great blessings...

Of my husband's new job after 448 days of waiting.

Living in an apartment for ten months while waiting for our Texas house to sell (even though I whined about waiting so long – forgive me, Lord!) During that time, we traveled on the weekends sight-seeing Idaho and the beauty of the state. And realizing all the things we would have missed had we stayed behind in Texas.

Here are just a few of the many blessings from the Lord.

Blessed with life in the Lord!

Blessed with knowing Jesus Christ as Savior.

Blessed with amazing times with God!

Blessed with a prayer, Bible study groups and a church home.

Blessed with friends who pursue God and love digging in His word.

Blessed with books, Bibles, and on-line study tools to bring me closer to God.

Blessed with mountains, rivers, botanical gardens, and the beauty of this area.

Blessed with provision for our every need and our wants.

Blessed with gorgeous sunrises and sunsets.

Blessed with road trips to see God's glory.

Blessed with eyes to see God's beauty!'

I remember Lord and praise You for Your blessings! I remember the great and amazing things You have done! And I am filled with joy!! Thank you, Father. Thank You!

Mining for Treasure

God has blessed you. What will you remember?

Take time to list your blessings.

~ *Want to get away?* ~

In Christ we find forgiveness.
In Christ we find mercy.
In Christ we find peace.
In Christ we find joy.
In Christ we find truth.
In Christ we find true riches.
In Christ we find eternal life.
In Christ we find all we need for every need.

Jesus Christ is The Way.

Mining for Treasure

Enjoy a getaway today with God. "My heart has heard you say, 'Come and talk with me.' And my heart responds, 'Lord, I am coming.'" ~ Psalm 27:8 (NLT)

~ Smash It! ~

In Judges 6-8, God equipped Gideon and his small army of 300 to battle against the Midianite army of over 100,000 men.

The weapons used by the Israelites? A torch, a pitcher, and a trumpet.

"Gideon and the hundred men with him reached the edge of the camp at the beginning of the middle watch, just after they had changed the guard. They blew their trumpets and broke the jars that were in their hands. The three companies blew the trumpets and smashed the jars. Grasping the torches in their left hands and holding in their right hands the trumpets they were to blow, they shouted, 'A sword for the Lord and for Gideon!' While each man held his position around the camp, all the Midianites ran, crying out as they fled." ~ Judges 7:19-21 (NIV)

The pitchers concealed the light of the torches, but once those pitchers were smashed, the light blazed forth and the enemy ran.

The enemy tries to cover God's light through fear, worry, whispers of past failures, condemnation, hopelessness, and futility.

You don't have to live in the dark. You don't have to walk in defeat.

No matter how big the problems, God is bigger. No matter how small or insignificant your weapons may seem, God's might is bigger.

Whatever you are up against, God's power is available to smash through the enemy's lies with the light of God's truth!

Mining for Treasure

Read God's truth, know God's truth, speak God's truth, and allow God's light to shine!

~ *Restoration* ~

I wonder, are some people struggling because they haven't prayed for those who wronged them?

There is power released when we pray for others – power to change us and power to release the power of God. "When Job prayed for his friends, the Lord restored his fortunes. In fact, the Lord gave him twice as much as before!" ~ Job 42:10 NLT

This morning as I pondered the verse in Job, God brought to mind the names of people who wronged me, names I had forgotten or blocked. They were names, faces, and situations that had been extremely harmful and difficult for me.

For in the releasing, forgiving, and praying for those people, they are not released from the wrongs committed, we are the ones released and blessed.

So, I brought each name, each face, each situation before God's throne asking that those who didn't know God that they would be blessed to know Him and receive Him as Lord and Savior.

When we bless others, when we pray for others, the blessings return and abound to restore our peace of mind, the fortune of knowing God better, and the amazing blessings of fellowship with Him. In praying for others, we are the ones who are blessed!

Need restoration? Pray, dear friends, pray, and watch the blessings flow.

Mining for Treasure

Do you need restoration? Has someone wronged you? Is there someone who comes to mind right now? Pray for them.

Is there someone you need to forgive? Pray for them. Pray for them, and watch the Lord restore you!

~ *True Hope* ~

Several years ago, the surgeon examined the raw, angry, eight-inch scar coursing down my hip. Tendons and ligaments had been cut, stretched, and sliced to rectify the damage, yet months had passed, and the area refused to heal. The physician's eyebrows rose as he made his announcement. "If improvement isn't seen in two months, we'll have to schedule you for further surgery."

The news was heart wrenching. No options were offered. No amount of medication took away the throbbing, maddening pain.

I slipped into my car and let the tears flow. For years my health and out of control immune system had become a constant source of frustration and pain. During that time every thought on God, man, life, and faith was turned upside down and shaken to their foundations. Tortured by pain and endless examinations of mind, body, and soul, I knew there had to be more to life.

An ember flickered and glowed as scripture came to mind. "This I recall to my mind, therefore I have hope, The Lord's loving kindnesses indeed never cease, for His compassions never fail. They are new every morning; great is Thy Faithfulness. The Lord is my portion ', says my soul, 'Therefore I have hope in Him'" ~ Lamentations 3:21-24 (NASB)

"I pray also that the eyes of your heart may be enlightened in order that you may know the hope to which He has called you, the riches of His glorious inheritance in the saints." ~ Ephesians 1:18 (NIV)

"Find rest, O my soul, in God alone; my hope comes from Him." ~ Psalm 62:5 (NIV)

"Lord, You are my hope. Lord, I have trusted You since I was young. I have depended on You since I was born; You helped me even on the day of my birth. I will always praise You." ~ Psalm 71:5-6 (NCV)

Hope is not found in the shifting sand of humanity but by focusing squarely on the might, depth, and vastness of a relationship with our Maker. Hope is enlightened by the inheritance freely offered by our Savior.

Through Jesus, we find true hope that refuses to be doused by pain and tears or extinguished by gale force winds. Hope is Heavenly based and Heavenly fed.

God's loving-kindness, compassion, and faithfulness are new every morning. He renews strength. He gives ability to walk through valleys and not grow weary—regardless of circumstances.

Precious one, hope is waiting. Hope that soars on wings of eagles, hope that becomes an unfailing treasure through pain and suffering. Hope found in Jesus Christ our eternal, forever hope ...The True Hope.

"But as for me, I will hope continually, and will praise You yet more and more." ~ Psalm 71:14 (NASB)

Mining for Treasure

Reading through the verses above, which one gave you greatest hope?

Hope is found throughout the Bible. Take the time write verses to remind you of the unfailing hope of God.

"Why am I discouraged? Why is my heart so sad? I will put my hope in God! I will praise him again—my Savior and my God!" ~ Psalm 42:11 (NLT)

~ Validate Me ~

We have a desire to be noticed. Some want fame and fortune, to see their name in lights, be on the big screen, or to top the music charts. Others long to publicly proclaim God's word. And even those who like to be behind the scenes want someone to recognize what they do and who they are.

Sometimes we strive to be noticed by "that" famous person, author, Bible teacher, singer, blogger, writer, speaker ... someone who will validate us or promote us. And yet when we pursue people for our validation, we will always come up lacking.

God, who is the God of the universe, can initiate any divine appointment. God notices. He sees you. He created you and loves you. His validation is far beyond what anyone on earth can ever do or say.

God, do You see me? Lord, do You watch and know what's happening? Do you think about me? Please still my heart. Please reassure me. Please let me know You are there. Please let me see beyond what I can see and whisper in my soul Your promises.

O my child, I see you and I know you. You are mine. My thoughts are always with you. Walk by faith, not by sight. Don't be afraid, I will never leave you or forsake you. I love you with an unfailing love. The mountains may depart and the hills be removed, but my steadfast love will never depart from you. My peace won't be removed and my compassion is with you, don't let your heart be troubled. Hold fast, you can't even imagine the good things I'm working out for you. I love you forever. ~ God

God's truth found in Isaiah 43:1, Psalm 139:17-18, 2 Corinthians 5:7, Deuteronomy 31:8, Psalm 33:5, Isaiah 54:10, John 14:2, 1 Corinthians 2:9, Matthew 6:34, Hebrews 10:23, Romans 8:28, Psalm 107:1

Mining for Treasure

Who do you seek for validation?
Dear friend, there is no situation you will face that God's tender eyes are not watching over you with love.
Remember God is the one who validates you. His love and affection outrank anyone and anything.
Seek Him above all things, and in all things, He will provide the validation you seek.

~ *Puppy Soul* ~

Our dog, bearing wisdom of years, retains a puppy soul. His sleep is filled with old dog snores, yet he plays with youthful vigor, and his eyes shine with loyal undying love.

When we return home, our little dog delivers wags, gifts, and jubilant dancing. My face and heart smile. He brings joy.

I wonder... do I also please God—my Master? What gifts do I bring Him?

What do you bring your Master?

Mining for Treasure

How can you bring joy today to God? Take a moment to thank Him and tell Him that you love Him?

Heavenly Father, help me always bring You joy. I long to make Your heart smile. You gift me beyond comprehension. You love me beyond my sins and cover me with Your mercy. Thank You, Father. You amaze me! You make my heart dance and sing! I love You, Father. Always and forever!

~ Hummingbird Moments ~

We've been blessed with small visitors in our yard. Hummingbirds flit, minuscule wings beating, microscopic-helicopters maneuvering with jet speed. With each glimpse of their tiny bodies, my heart thrills.

I don't want to miss the hummingbird moments. I want eyes to see blessings that whoosh into our lives straight from God's love.

> The love of God.
> The sacrifice of Jesus Christ for our sins.
> The blessings of breath and life.
> The laugh of a baby.
> The butterfly that lingers.
> The smile of a stranger.
> The purr of a kitten.
> The wagging tail of a dog.
> The flower that blooms.
> The hummingbird moments of joy.

Heavenly Father help me to live every day and every moment with the spirit of excitement. Oh, that I would thrill to watch for what You graciously provide and reveal.

Mining for Treasure

Watch for God's joyful hummingbird moments. The more you watch for them, the more you will notice.

~ *What If We Truly Believed?* ~

What if we truly believed? What if ***I truly believed?*** What if I let go of the plans and worries of tomorrow's bank account, health, and social interactions, to interact with THE ONE who has the plans, who has our health in the palm of His hands, who is my provider, who is The One I need to have, long to have, MUST have. He is the One, THE ONLY ONE who fills my soul's emptiness.

I'll admit, I don't think I dream big enough. I forget how BIG and AMAZING our God is, and how He uses weak humans in His divine plans. Oh, to come to Him with the faith of a child, bright-eyed in wonder, ready to do whatever He calls us to do, ready to dream **BIG**.

It's fun to visualize safe in God's arms, holding hands with my sisters and brothers-in-Christ, and leaping fearlessly into the plans God has for us. O what joy if we would all encourage, love on one another, and believe, truly believe, the amazing things that God has planned.

Also remember that those BIG plans may be small in our eyes — from the love we give to our family members and friends, or it could be allowing the Holy Spirit free reign to work in us and through us in home and abroad.

God is a BIG God with BIG plans!

Let's never hinder God. So, let's truly believe. Let's believe God — THE ONE who finds nothing impossible. The Creator of the universe, The One who loves with an unfailing love, The One who knows the plans He has for us, The One who is All in All.

Let's believe God!

"'For I know the plans that I have for you,' declares the Lord, 'plans for welfare and not for calamity to give you a future and a hope.'" ~ Jeremiah 29:11 (NASB)

Mining for Treasure

Believing God results in the power of God.

Will you believe?

~ Who Is God to You? ~

Who is God?
Who is your God?
Is He God when He answers your prayers?
Is He God when He does your bidding?
Is He God when you get the job, house, car,
or person you want?
Do you love God for what He does or who He is?

Is He God when your answers don't come?
Is He God when the answer is "no"?
Is He still your God when you don't get the job, the house,
the car, or the person you want?

Is He still God?
Is He still your God?

Oh, Father God, whatever may come,
You are my God forever and always.

Mining for Treasure

Please don't allow circumstances to alter the truth of who God truly is. God's love is unfailing regardless of whatever you are going through or whatever you face.

~ I AM ~

"Do not fear, for I am with you; do not be dismayed, for I am your God. I will strengthen you and help you; I will uphold you with my righteous right hand."
~ Isaiah 41:10 (NIV)

I know what you need.
I will provide what you need.
I will be all you need.
I am what you need.
I will protect you.
I am your shield.
I am your deliverer.
I am your salvation.
I am truth.
I am hope.
I am unfailing love.
I am for you.
I am with you.
I am the way.
I am life.
I am truth.
I am The One who made you, loves you, comforts you, protects you, will never leave or forsake you.

I AM ~ God

Mining for Treasure

God is The I Am, which means He is already present for every moment of our lives.

~ Gap Seeker ~

Will you stand in the gap for your family, your home, your job, for others? God is seeking for those who will stand in the gap. "I looked for someone who might rebuild the wall of righteousness that guards the land. I searched for someone to stand in the gap in the wall so I wouldn't have to destroy the land, but I found no one." ~ Ezekiel 22:30 (NLT)

Will you pray for the city and country where God has sent you, seeking His best? Jeremiah 29:7 reminds us to seek the peace and the prosperity of the city where God has sent you. Charles Spurgeon wrote, "The man who is mighty in prayer may be a wall of fire around his country, her guardian angel and her shield."

Will you pray for those in ministry, that God will open hearts to receive His salvation? Charles Spurgeon relates the following, "A certain preacher, whose sermons converted men by scores, received a revelation from heaven that not one of the conversions was owing to his talents or eloquence, but all to the prayers of an illiterate lay-brother, who sat on the pulpit steps pleading all the time for the success of his sermons."

Will you fight the enemy in prayer? Prayers with passion for God's purpose, fueled with Godly determination, battle back the enemy. The power of prayer is mighty and powerful!

Will you be the one who stands in the gap, seeking God's best for your environment, praying for those in ministry, and fight the good fight to beat down the enemy's obstacles? The enemy is busy trying to get inside, make inroads, destroy people, cities, ministries, and families, will you be one who stands in the gap?

Mining for Treasure

Stand in the gap for others. Your prayers make a difference in your life, your family, your country, and the world.

Please stand in the gap.

~ Feeted Faith ~

Proclaiming a strong faith is much easier than truly living a strong faith. When trials and difficulties come, we are given the opportunity to put feet to our faith. It's not just talking about our faith but walking out our faith. It's standing firm during those nasty trials of life.

God has blessed us with another opportunity to not just walk by sight but walk by faith. And I'll be honest, it's not always easy. But I know my redeemer lives. I know God will be faithful because <u>God is faithful</u>.

I can look back and see all the amazing ways He has provided, rescued, and redeemed every single nasty thing the enemy has tried to mess up.

So, we are choosing to rejoice, choosing to believe and trust, and choosing to keep our feet firmly planted in faith.

Join me?

"Be on the alert, stand firm in the faith. For we walk by faith, not by sight" ~ 1 Corinthians 16:13, 2 Corinthians 5:7 (NASB)

Mining for Treasure

God blesses with spiritual armor to help through our life journey. To stand firm and walk with feeted faith, keep the Good News of peace firmly on your feet!

"So, stand strong, with the belt of truth tied around your waist and the protection of right living on your chest. On your feet wear the Good News of peace to help you stand strong." ~ Ephesians 6:14-15 (NCV)

~ *Pulled Apart* ~

Unending needs, wants, and desires of others constantly clamors and claws for attention. The world, people, friends, family, work, and the busyness of the day, threaten to pull the soul apart.

Jesus understands. With friends, family, followers, and all the needs/wants/desires of the world clamored for His attention, yet Jesus never hurried. He took time, made time, to be with His Father.

Jesus intentionally stayed focused on His Father's agenda. The world, people, friends, family pulled on Him, but His driving force, His only pull He allowed to pull was His Father.

Being in the presence of God the Father is the only place, the only presence, which aligns all the pieces that are pulled apart.

Soul stressed?

In God's presence all the pieces pulled apart become properly aligned.

"Are you tired? Worn out? Burned out on religion? Come to me. Get away with me and you'll recover your life. I'll show you how to take a real rest. Walk with me and work with me—watch how I do it. Learn the unforced rhythms of grace. I won't lay anything heavy or ill-fitting on you. Keep company with me and you'll learn to live freely and lightly." ~ Matthew 11:28-30 (MSG)

Mining for Treasure

Whatever is pulling you apart, take that to God, and He will put you back together again.

~ *Remember to Tell Them* ~

During a time of difficulty, fervent prayers flew to heaven and prayer requests were sent to friends and family. A month later an unexpected blessing of provision arrived. We sat stunned, giddy, amazed, and grateful.

Yet I found myself hesitating to share, hesitating because I was unsure of the reaction of friends and family who struggle with so many needs. However, if I am only faithful to share requests of the hard things and not share God's answers and His goodness, I'm not being fair to others or to God.

Don't allow your fears or the enemy silence what God is doing and how He is working. Share the prayer requests but also share the answers.

I realize some may not rejoice and some may be jealous, but please don't allow someone else's reaction (or non-reaction) stop you from sharing the good things God is doing in your life. And yes, there is a time and place. There is a time to rejoice with those who rejoice and weep with those who weep. Be appropriate.

But please remember to tell others what God has done, how He answered your prayers, how He provides, because we all need hope. We all need to hear how God works, because sometimes answers don't seem to come, or take SO very long, we need to hear and remember God's faithfulness.

Bolster, encourage, and help others remember God's faithfulness. **Remember to tell them what God has done!** Tell them how much the Lord has done for you.

Mining for Treasure

Will you tell others what God has done in your life?

Share how God has helped you through a difficult time, or how He has blessed, or how He is carrying you through heartache and pain.

As you share you will bless others and receive the blessings of voicing praise for our wonderful God.

~ *Traveling Light* ~

There are times I imagine living in a little cabin in the woods with the bare minimum. Okay, not too bare, but most of what is in our home we could do without -- pictures, furniture, and things we have brought with us from move to move.

Some objects have a special attachment because friends or family gave them, but most of our stuff is just stuff. So very little is actually needed for our daily existence. I wonder how often lives are heavy with the weight of possessions?

The less we have, the less we have to clean, the less to watch over or worry about, the less insurance and storage space.

Oswald Chambers reminds us, "When Jesus Christ talked about discipleship, He indicated that a disciple must be detached from property and possessions, for if a man's life is in what he possesses, when disaster comes to his possessions, his life goes too."

As Christians, we are to travel light. Personally, traveling heavy is not an appealing notion. Jesus said His yoke is easy and His burden light. (Matthew 11:30)

Freedom is experienced when who we are, what we are, is found in Christ -- not in what we have. "Why do you spend money for that which is not bread? And why do you work for what does not satisfy? Come to Me, and eat what is good, and let your soul delight itself in fatness. Incline your ear, and come to Me; hear, and your soul will live." ~ Isaiah 55:2-3 (NASB)

God promises blessings -- abundant blessings -- His blessings. Nothing will satisfy and complete, but Him.

I'm thinking of traveling light. Want to join me?

Mining for Treasure

What changes could you make to help you travel light?

~ *Be Available* ~

It is God who prepares the way, the listening ear, the open heart. It is God who opens blind eyes and unlocks souls to receive His message. It is God who draws people to His heart.

What joy for those who will be a willing vessel to say what God wants said, to share Him, and then to watch how He works.

Be available to be used by God. In your words, your life, and your actions, be available to watch God work.

We are messengers, He is the Savior.

Be available to watch the amazing ways God works in lives when you are available.

God use us.
Use us to spread Your love.
Use us to touch lives for You.
Use us to be Your hands and feet.
Use us to tell a hurting world about Your compassion.
Use us to enlighten those who are kept in darkness.
Use us to share with others Your blessings.
Use us to reveal Your grace and mercy to those lost in sin.
Use us to tell the stories of how You rescued us.
Use us for Your glory.
Heavenly Father, we make ourselves available to You,
please use us!

Mining for Treasure

What is your heart's cry to God? Take a moment to pray how you would like Him to use you.

~ *Desire and Longing* ~

Often there is something stirring within us, a passion that drives to distraction. We think we know what is needed – "that" job, "that" spouse, "that" house, "that" car, "that" amount of money, "that" child, "that" possession, "that" ....

But have you asked God? Have you asked Him how to fill that empty spot, that desire, want, or need?

Do you have a desire and longing? Ask God how He wants that fulfilled. Ask God where your eyes should be looking, where your soul should be focused.

Ask God. Spend time with Him. Spend time with His Word. Listen. Cease striving. Rest. And as you curl into His presence, the answers will come. The guidance will be revealed. The longing will be directed and satisfied.

Ask God. He's waiting for you. "Call to Me and I will answer you and will tell you great and hidden things that you have not known. And I will give you treasures hidden in the darkness – secret riches. I will do this so you may know that I am the Lord, the God of Israel, the one who calls you by name." ~ Jeremiah 33:3 (NASB), Isaiah 45:3 (NLT)

Mining for Treasure

Whatever desire and longings are in your heart, give them to God and allow Him to fill you.

~ *Standing Faith* ~

The image is burned in my mind. A man and his wife sit in the dirt in a refugee camp. When the rebels came, the family with their six children left with nothing but the clothes on their back.

Nothing.
No possessions.
No home.
Nothing.

The one thing the man asked for, his only request? A Bible.

A Bible to preach God's word to other refuges. A Bible to share God's hope. This man, a pastor, lost everything, but his faith remains.

How is your faith? Does it stand strong only on "good" days? Or does your faith waver during trials and tribulation? Would you still love God, still serve Him, if you lost everything?

No matter what happened in the past, no matter what happens in the future, will your faith stand firmly on God's truth?

God's Truth won't desert you.
God's Truth watches over you.
God's Truth knows no bounds.
God's Truth is eternal.
God's Truth is unfailing love.

Whatever happens, will you stand firm on His Truth?

"Even though the fig trees have no blossoms, and there are no grapes on the vines; even though the olive crop fails, and the fields lie empty and barren; even though the flocks die in the fields, and the cattle barns are empty, yet I will rejoice in the Lord! I will be joyful in the God of my salvation! I came naked from my mother's womb, and I will be naked when I leave. The Lord gave me what I had, and the Lord has taken it away. Praise the name of the Lord! Whom have I in heaven but you? I desire you more than anything on earth." ~ Habakkuk 3:17-18, Job 1:21, Psalm 73:25 (NLT)

Mining for Treasure

Every day we are given opportunities to stand firm in our faith. Every choice we make, every action we take, shows our level of faith.

Remember God's truth, study His word, and hold fast to His promises.

God will hold you steady and help you faithfully stand through every situation you encounter.

~ *Know Whose Light to Follow* ~

Have you ever noticed an animal standing in the middle of the road at night? The car lights mesmerize and draw them forward or cause them to stand still with their jaw hanging open. I want to hang my head out of the window and warn them to stay away from the light.

Unfortunately, many times life's temptations attract us like shiny objects, and we aren't any smarter than a bug winging its way to a bug zapper.

We need to know Whose light to follow.

Jesus said, He is the light of the world. Whoever follows Him won't walk in darkness but will have the light of life (John 8:12).

Keep your focus by knowing God's word, knowing His truth, and fixing your eyes on The True Light—Jesus Christ.

Mining for Treasure

Rest in the wonderful truth that God has blessed you, through Christ, to have the light of knowledge for your life's journey. "For God, who said, 'Let light shine out of darkness,' made His light shine in our hearts to give us the light of the knowledge of the glory of God in the face of Christ." ~ 2 Corinthians 4:6 (NASB)

Always look to His light for every step of the way. His word is a lamp for your feet and a light for your path. (Psalm 119:105)

~ *Running* ~

I didn't know how to stop running. If the phone rang, I ran to make sure I answered. If someone sent me a message, an email, a tweet, or a comment, I ran to answer and thank.

If someone had a birthday on Facebook, I wanted to make sure they knew I cared. 5000 Facebook friends kept me jumping.

Then God whispered in my spirit to pull away. And I did. My page was changed where I no longer saw everyone else's updates. I could no longer visit anyone else's page. I was quarantined to my own.

My time was so occupied with people, I had lost time with God. All my running to answer everyone's comments left me without time to hear from God.

All my running to "help" others caused me to run from The One who is The help. I had forgotten my place in the race of life, I had forgotten to fix my eyes on Jesus, the help people really need.

Yes, I can be kind, caring, and love others, but my main purpose and goal is to point to Jesus Christ – The Savior.

Changes were made in my online interactions. And slowly, beautifully, my soul stopped running. My heart found rhythm with Him.

The world didn't fall apart and all the broken pieces in my soul were put back together as I rested in God's tender care.

And the amazing blessing was that God actually blessed with more growth in my ministry. Because as I pursued only Him, He gave me more time to accomplish all He required.

Mining for Treasure

Do you feel like you are running ragged? Please don't get in the trap I found myself. Don't allow the concern for what others think of you to pull you away from time with God.

If you are running, make sure you are running only after God.

~ *The "Good News" Channel* ~

One glance at the world news is enough to give the average person heartburn and a restless night's sleep. I appreciate the news channels, but boy, wouldn't it be nice to have a "good news" channel? Only the good news would be reported, like ...

> Across the world, loving parents care for children.
> People reach out to help those in need.
> Rescued kitties and puppies given to good homes.
> Innocent laughter of children bring delight to listening ears.
> Sinners saved by God's grace rejoice in their new lives.
> Broken hearts and lives mended and restored.

The headlines above may not be broadcast across the airwaves, but they are true. However, the enemy wants us to see the evil and the bad in the world and in others, ignoring anything good and focusing on hopelessness and futility.

The more we center our attention on the negative, the more we become disillusioned and ineffective. Are you spending more time watching the news, reading or listening to the news of the world, above reading God's Good News?

There is not a moment we are not surrounded by God's love and goodness. Don't let the enemy blind you to the truth—good things do happen, good people do exist, and God is working throughout our world. And every moment of every day, God beckons us to spend time with Him and His word. God really does have a Good News Channel. Open the Bible and read the best news ever — God's Good News!

"Summing it all up, friends, I'd say you'll do best by filling your minds and meditating on things true, noble, reputable, authentic, compelling, gracious—the best, not the worst; the beautiful, not the ugly; things to praise, not things to curse." ~ Philippians 4:8 MSG.

Heavenly Father, open the eyes of my heart and filter my thoughts through Your truth. Help me to focus on the proper praising perspective and keep spreading Your good news!

Mining for Treasure

With the constant stream of bad news, please make a constant effort to be careful what you listen to and what is watched. For what is fed into the soul either shrivels, rots, or nourishes.

Paul warns us, "Do not participate in the unfruitful deeds of darkness, but instead even expose them; for it is disgraceful even to speak of the things which are done by them in secret." ~Ephesians 5:11-12 (NASB)

How can you guard your mind and help bring good news to your heart and the world around you?

~ Stuffed ~

What if today someone called and told you that you had a wonderful new job and a new place in a different city, but you have two days to report. The dream job and benefits are waiting for you, but you have to move yourself. You can't use someone to help. Only you and your family can pack and move your objects.

Would you panic? (Boy I would!) How long would it take to prepare the house, how much clutter would need to be removed? Could it be done?

At times I wonder what it would be like to start fresh. How many possessions would I accumulate this time around?

Earthly wealth won't last for eternity. The more stuff we have, the more time is required to care for, clean, protect, and maintain that stuff. Stuff will knock the stuffing out of us.

I don't want to be stuffed. And as a person whose name is Buffaloe, that could take on many different meanings. Ack!

The only thing I want filling my life, is what will last for eternity. I want my soul stuffed with God's love.

O what freedom we can hold when we let go of the things of this world. The more we place into God's hands, the more we receive. "But seek first His kingdom and His righteousness; and all these things shall be added to you." Matthew 6:33

God's ways, God's wisdom, offers us treasures beyond anything we can imagine. "Riches and honor are mine to give. So are wealth and lasting success. What I give is better than the finest gold, better than the purest silver. I do what is right and follow the path of justice. I give wealth to those who love me, filling their houses with treasures." ~Proverbs 8:18-21 (NCV)

Mining for Treasure

Is there anything in your life that needs to be cleaned out?

Unstuff the stuff so you may be stuffed with the beauty of God's treasures!

~ Leaking eyes ~

"... Every night my bed is wet with tears; my bed is soaked from my crying." ~ Psalm 6:6 (NCV)

Years ago, I flew from Chicago to Texas to be with my brother Lee and sister-in-law, Kathy. She was my best friend and now terminally ill with leukemia in the hospital. Their daughter Kelly was only a toddler.

Kelly needed clothes so I took their car to a store to purchase a few things. When I came out, I could not find the vehicle -- worse yet, I couldn't even remember what the car looked like.

I wandered up and down the parking lot searching, praying, and trying to recall the make, color, and model. What if the car had been stolen?

My emotions were raw from watching Kathy suffer. You know those times you think if one more thing happens you are going to fall over the edge of sanity? I was close.

I prayed and hoped everyone in the store would finish shopping and claim their cars so I could take the last one left. Finally, while peeking in windows; I noticed something in a car that looked familiar. The key fit and I collapsed in the front seat in tears.

Another dear friend was heartbroken as one of her grown children made choices that were breaking her heart. So, she waits and prays for God's protection. She said it makes her eyes leak.

Another friend visits her husband at the nursing home. God miraculously healed him from his first stroke. The second stroke was different. She never knew what a new day would bring, making life frightening and confusing for them both. Some days her husband is so far away. Yet there was a special day, he was with her, really with her, and he sang to her, "You are my sunshine." Her eyes leak as she waits, hopes, and prays, clinging to the arms of her Heavenly Father.

There is so much pain, disappointment, and frustration in this life on earth. The tears, sobs, and leaking eyes, tie us to our human nature. We are frightened children unable to see the future; all we know is yesterday and today with its sorrow and suffering.

The agony is beyond words and in our fear and frustration, we cry out to God. Blessed hope is found in the verse... "The Spirit helps us in our weakness. We do not know what we ought to pray for, but the Spirit himself intercedes for us with groans that words cannot express." ~ Romans 8:26 (NIV)

The Lord knows the significance of each tear, and every drop is noted, recorded and precious. "You number my wanderings; Put my tears into Your bottle; are they not in Your book?" ~ Psalm 56:7-8 (NKJV) Your tears are never ignored, and with each drop our Heavenly Father promises He is with you.

There may be wandering times through the parking lot of life sobbing, or struggling through difficulties as eyes leak from pain, but God will grant enough strength, enough love, and enough grace for one more day. "The Lord also will be a refuge for the oppressed, A refuge in times of trouble. And those who know Your name will put their trust in You; For You, Lord, have not forsaken those who seek You." ~ Psalm 9:9-10 (NKJV)

And every new day He promises He will never leave us, never for a moment. Through the pain, within His arms, we will be safe, held close and loved. He will help us through, and He will guide us home. Safely home -- our ultimate home -- His home and our home forever where there will be no more crying, pain, or tears.

"He will wipe every tear from their eyes. There will be no more death or mourning or crying or pain, for the old order of things has passed away." ~ Revelation 21:4 (NIV)

Mining for Treasure

Please always remember God cares for you. He cares when you hurt. His heart is tender and loving toward His children and every tear you cry is precious to Him.

~ *Warning Labels* ~

"While you were doing all these things, declares the LORD, I spoke to you again and again, but you did not listen; I called you, but you did not answer." ~ Jeremiah 7:13 (NIV)

Our puppy relaxed on the floor, then as though without warning, his tail wagged. He turned his head and stared at the furry object waving back and forth. The tail stopped and dropped to the floor. Over and over this scenario played out... the wag, the stare, the tail drop. Finally, he pounced. The tail didn't stand a chance.

He no longer chases his tail, but when he gets in trouble, he scowls at his tail as though the tail was the one who led him astray. You cannot trust a tail.

Sound familiar? The blame game started at the dawn of time. Adam and Eve played this game. Remember when they were "caught" by God? Adam immediately blamed Eve, who blamed the snake, and the snake didn't have a leg to stand on.

My parents taught me right from wrong and how to live a Godly life. Yet I still at times chose to ignore their advice. And I can tell 'ya every bad choice I made came with negative consequences.

The Bible is filled with God's love, and with His love come warnings and directions. Many people want to accept God's love but decline His commandments.

God lovingly warns us to avoid certain dangers. When a road sign says, "Bridge out ahead" driving without stopping will result in unsightly consequences.

God doesn't put parameters on our life as punishment, but for our protection and safety. He knows the tragic outcome of disobedience, and He knows the beautiful results of obedience.

One morning, while putting in my contacts, I accidently chose the cleaner instead of the wetting solution. The contact stuck on my eye causing the cleaning solution to work deep and leave a nasty chemical burn. I'm talking one major ouch.

I can't blame anyone but myself. The warning labels were there, the bottle signaled danger. Unfortunately, because of my carelessness, being distracted—not paying attention to that bright red bottle with the big warning sticker, I had some nasty consequences.

When God tells us to not do something, He is not taking away our freedom—He is giving us freedom from sin and death, freedom to live under His grace, and freedom to experience eternal life.

The Psalmist reminds us... "I will obey your teachings forever and ever. So, I will live in freedom, because I want to follow your orders."~ Psalm 119:44 (NCV)

Think about the freedoms we are given by God's laws. If everyone on this planet honestly and truly lived by the Ten Commandments we wouldn't have to worry about being lied to, murdered, or having anything stolen, the Sabbath would truly be a day of rest and relaxation, and every facet of our life would be better.

James tells us, "Do what God's teaching says; when you only listen and do nothing, you are fooling yourselves. Those who hear God's teaching and do nothing are like people who look at themselves in a mirror. They see their faces and then go away and quickly forget what they looked like but the truly happy people are those who carefully study God's perfect law that makes people free, and they continue to study it. They do not forget what they heard, but they obey what God's teaching says. Those who do this will be made happy." ~ James 1:22-25 (NCV)

"So be careful and do not refuse to listen when God speaks. Others refused to listen to Him when He warned them on earth, and they did not escape. So, it will be worse for us if we refuse to listen to God who warns us from heaven." ~ Hebrews 12:25-26 (NCV)

Mining for Treasure

Will you make the choice to live under God's loving direction?

Jesus said, "If you love Me, you will obey what I command." ~ John 14:15

~ *Do you really know?* ~

I've been pondering these two verses. "My people are destroyed from lack of knowledge..." ~ Hosea 4:6 (NIV) and "...but the people who know their God shall prove themselves strong and shall stand firm and do exploits [for God]. ~ Daniel 11:32 (AMP)

Are we being destroyed by the enemy, living ineffective lives, and not accomplishing strong exploits for God because we don't know God?

Not surface knowledge but knowing God and His character. Knowing who He is, His all-encompassing authority, His amazing strength, power, mercy, and love, knowing our allegiance to stand firm, and having a hunger and drive for the true knowledge of God.

Do we spend time in His word to foster a relationship of listening and obeying? Are we willing to dive into a deep, abiding knowledge of God?

I want to be like Paul and say, "I know (perceive, have knowledge of, and am acquainted with) Him Whom I have believed (adhered to and trusted in and relied on), and I am [positively] persuaded that He is able to guard and keep that which has been entrusted to me and which I have committed [to Him]. ~ 2 Timothy 1:12 (AMP)

Times are changing. True Christianity does not live in the gray. We must go beyond the thoughts, ideals, and views on being a good person, religious, or spiritual.

We have to know Who we know. Know Who we believe, and know our salvation is secure through Jesus Christ. We must know so we may spread the Good News of freedom to those who are held in captivity by the enemy.

Know God and seek His face. The more you know God, the greater the freedom, the firmer the foundation, the more fruit bearing, and the more radical, joy-filled, exploit living life!

"Because of this, since the day we heard about you, we have continued praying for you, asking God that you will know fully what he wants. We pray that you will also have great wisdom and understanding in spiritual things so that you will live the kind of life that honors and pleases the Lord in every way. You will produce fruit in every good work and grow in the knowledge of God." ~ Colossians 1:9-10 (NCV)

Mining for Treasure

Unfortunately, many of us have more knowledge about celebrities or sports teams than God's word. I have read many books by different authors, glimpsing into their lives, but I do not have a personal relationship with them. Knowing their words and truly knowing them in a one-on-one relationship is different.

Pursue God through His words in the Bible, seek Him with your heart, spend time talking with Him, quietly sitting at His feet. For when you seek to know, you will know.

"Ask, and it will be given to you; seek, and you will find; knock, and it will be opened to you. For everyone who asks receives, and he who seeks finds, and to him who knocks it will be opened." ~ Matthew 7:7-8 (NKJV)

~ *Laying Stones* ~

My sweet husband and I viewed The Truth Project at a friend's house. One topic on the DVD discussed history and the attempts by some to revise historical truth. One of the things they mentioned is that History is HIS story.

So that makes me ponder.

We are all here for a purpose, and that purpose does not just encompass only ourselves. The picture is broader, bigger, and more than we can imagine. There is more at stake than only our story and existence. Our lives, our history, our legacy, leaves foundations and stepping stones for those who will come behind us.

So, my questions for myself and for you: ...

What foundations are you laying for others?

Are you laying stepping stones for those who come behind you?

Will your steps lead them straight to Christ?

What stones are you laying?

Mining for Treasure

What stones can you leave for those who will follow?

"When your children ask their fathers in time to come, what do these stones mean? You shall let your children know; Israel came over this Jordan on dry ground. For the Lord your God dried up the waters of the Jordan for you until you passed over, as the Lord your God did to the Red Sea, which He dried up for us until we passed over." ~ Joshua 4:21-23 (NIV)

~ *Surface Scratchers* ~

I enjoy watching the California Quail that visit our bird feeder. They look so cute with their little plumed hats and serious expressions.

What I find humorous is how they lift their heads while their little feet scratch the ground. They don't even watch to see what they're stirring up.

I think during my early life I was a human Quail. I grew up in the church. My dad was in the ministry, and my mom sang in the choir with her beautiful soprano voice. I carried my little Bible, and I could even rattle off a few verses. I thought I knew God's word, but all I was doing was scratching the surface.

I'm no longer satisfied just knowing a few scriptures; I want to know the heart of God. Because the more we read and study God's word, the more we obey and put God's truth into practice, the deeper our footing. And then when the storms of life hit, we are held firm by the solid foundation of The Solid Rock.

Jesus said, "I will show you what he is like who comes to me and hears my words and puts them into practice. He is like a man building a house, who dug down deep and laid the foundation on rock. When a flood came, the torrent struck that house but could not shake it, because it was well built." ~ Luke 6:47-48 (NIV)

Join me in prayer?

Dear Heavenly Father, I want to not only read and hear Your words but put them into practice. Help me not to only scratch at the surface, but to build a solid foundation on Your word so that I'm forever safe in You.

Mining for Treasure

Are you like the Quail that only scratch the surface?
Please take time to dig deep into God's word and put them into practice. The blessings will be amazing!

~ Solid Foundation ~

Reaching 2722 feet into the air, the world's tallest manmade structure is the Burj Khalifa tower in Dubai. Over 58,900 cubic yards of concrete were used to construct the concrete and steel foundation along with 192 piles buried more than 164 feet deep. And still there are reports the building is sinking in the sandy soil.

No matter how deep the foundation, without a solid base there is danger of sinking. In the same way, if we don't build our lives on the solid rock of Jesus Christ, there will be trouble ahead.

In Webster's 1828 Dictionary, "Rock" is defined as defense; means of safety; protection; strength; asylum. Firmness; a firm or immovable foundation.

Every day the news reports killings, natural disasters, wars, and suffering. I'm not going to tell you that Christianity equals earthly safety. No, Christianity is so much more. Christianity leads to soul-security, soul-safety, and a personal relationship that walks with you through every bit of the good, the bad, and the ugly.

There is no solid ground without Christ. There is no soul-safety without Christ. There is nothing secure enough to be eternally secure without Christ. The only rock forever firm is the rock -- Jesus Christ.

Our world may be shaken, but our souls remain solid in the foundation of our Lord and Savior, Jesus Christ.

Mining for Treasure

What have you built on as your foundation for now and the future?

"The people who know their God shall stand firm." -- Daniel 11:32

"Now it is God who makes both us and you stand firm in Christ..." ~, 2 Corinthians 1:21 (NIV)

"The Lord is exalted, for he dwells on high; he will fill Zion with his justice and righteousness. He will be the sure foundation for your times, a rich store of salvation and wisdom and knowledge; the fear of the Lord is the key to this treasure." ~ Isaiah 33:5-6 (NIV)

Jesus said, "I will show you what it's like when someone comes to me, listens to my teaching, and then follows it. It is like a person building a house who digs deep and lays the foundation on solid rock. When the floodwaters rise and break against that house, it stands firm because it is well built. But anyone who hears and doesn't obey is like a person who builds a house without a foundation. When the floods sweep down against that house, it will collapse into a heap of ruins." ~ Luke 6:47-49 (NLT)

~ *Rock the World* ~

The followers and disciples of Jesus had their world rocked when he was crucified. Huddled together they were scared, questioning, and uncertain of their future. Until the resurrected Savior walked back into their world and rocked them out of their fear.

Once too timid and afraid to leave the room, they now knew the truth. Jesus Christ was, and is, alive! And because they knew, because they were sure of what they had seen and heard, those few told the world about Jesus, and they rocked the world.

On the solid rock we too can rock the world. Rocking and rolling through life, we can share God's love.

One little rock can start an avalanche. One little rock can ripple to distant shores. One little rock standing on the Solid Rock, can rock the world.

Let's rock the world for Jesus!

Mining for Treasure

How can you rock the world for Christ?

~ To Those Who Overcome ~

"He who overcomes, I will grant to him to sit down with Me on My throne, as I also overcame and sat down with My Father on His throne." ~ Revelation 3:21 (NASB)

Being the only female in the house, you can be assured I am "privileged" to view many military shows. Recently we watched the Navy SEAL training course, considered to the toughest in the world by military experts. The training is intense and grueling, pushing the recruits to their physical and mental limits.

During one of their many long, long, long, long runs, the instructors followed in a truck repeatedly reminding the recruits how tired they must be and how much pain they must be in. The instructors don't want any man to be part of their team that can't work through the physical and mental fatigue. They want men who can push deep into themselves to squeeze out every ounce of courage and strength they possess.

Why do these men voluntarily endure months and months of agonizing training? Because they know if they complete the course, they will become privileged to be part of one of the finest military units in the country.

Life is difficult. There are days we feel at the end of our rope, body and mind exhausted without strength to move another inch. Don't you find it interesting that you can hear the enemy so loudly with reminders of the pain and frustration? Satan does not want us to succeed—he wants our failure.

Peter warns us, "Control yourselves and be careful! The devil, your enemy, goes around like a roaring lion looking for someone to eat. Refuse to give in to him, by standing strong in your faith. You know that your Christian family all over the world is having the same kinds of suffering. And after you suffer for a short time, God, who gives all grace, will make everything right. He will make you strong and support you and keep you from falling. He called you to share in his glory in Christ, a glory that will continue forever." ~ 1 Peter 5:8-10 (NCV)

Just as every phase of the SEAL training has a purpose and a goal, our Heavenly Father will never give you more than you can handle, and He will never allow you to go through something that will not have a greater good.

When life gets difficult, don't give up, don't quit, and don't listen to the enemy. Don't allow doubts to overwhelm you and lose your victory. Never give up. Fight the good fight of the faith. Take hold of the eternal life to which you were called. Be on your guard; stand firm in the faith; be courageous; be strong. Be strong in the Lord and in His mighty power.

You can be victorious and overcome with the help of our Savior, with the might of His hand and the strength of His Spirit. The overcomers are ones who believe that Jesus is the Son of God. Be an overcomer!

Mining for Treasure

The word of the Lord tells us that there is much victory when we overcome the difficulties in our lives.

Read through the verses below and remember no matter what the enemy is yelling in your ear, keep pressing on to overcome.

The one who overcomes, "I will give the right to eat from the tree of life, which is in the paradise of God." ~ Revelation 2:7 (NASB)

The one who overcomes "will not be hurt at all by the second death." ~ Revelation 2:11 (NASB)

To the one who overcomes "I will give some of the hidden manna, and I will give him a white stone, and a new name written on the stone which no one knows but he who receives it." ~ Revelation 2:17 (NASB)

The one who overcomes, "(is victorious) and who obeys My commands to the [very] end [doing the works that please Me], I will give him authority and power over the nations." ~ Revelation 2:26 (AMP)

The one who overcomes, "I will never blot out the name of that person from the book of life but will acknowledge that name before my Father and his angels." ~ Revelation 3:5 (NIV)

To the one who overcomes, "I will grant to him to sit down with Me on My throne, as I also overcame and sat down with My Father on His throne." ~ Revelation 3:21 (NASB)

Keep fighting for the goal, keep pushing forward and ignore the enemy's taunts, because the rewards are great for those who overcome.

He who overcomes will inherit all this, "and I will be their God and they will be my children." ~ Revelation 21:7 (NIV)

Will you be an overcomer?

~ Weight Lifting ~

My husband and I met at a gym where we both lifted weights. The process was fun and exciting to watch strained muscles become sculpted and strong. For motivation and safety, a spotter would be required during the lifting of heavy weights.

Any help, verbally or physically, given during the repetitions, increased my strength. And the stronger my helper, the less concern I had during the process.

In the same way, God helps us with each trial and difficulty. Our spiritual muscles and faith will grow at an amazing rate when we allow Him to help with every "weight" the world throws our way. We never lift them alone.

George Muller writes of trials, "If the Lord left me to myself, one tenth of the difficulties and trials I face would be enough to overwhelm me. But as long as He sustains me, I am carried through one difficulty after another. By God's help I would be able to bear other difficulties and trials. I expect an increase of faith with every fresh difficulty the Lord helps me through

So, remember to "Cast your burden on the Lord **[releasing the weight of it]** and He will sustain you; He will never allow the [consistently] righteous to be moved (made to slip, fall, or fail). Have I not commanded you? Be strong and courageous. Do not be afraid; do not be discouraged, for the Lord your God will be with you wherever you go." ~ Psalm 55:22 (AMP), Joshua 1:9 (NIV)

Mining for Treasure

The Psalmist tells us to cast the weight of our burdens on the Lord, and casting is an active process. Jesus said in

Matthew 6 -- do not worry. God knows what you need, seek Him first and He will take care of the rest, and do not worry about tomorrow because tomorrow will worry about its own things.

I have to chuckle when I think about the statement. I don't need to worry about tomorrow, because when tomorrow comes it is today, and with today is another tomorrow, and tomorrow is already gone because it is today.... Oh, how clever our Lord! Give all those worries to Him, every single one of them. Cast the worry weight on the strong, loving shoulders of Christ!

Remember to "Cast all your anxiety on Him because He cares for you." ~ 1 Peter 5:7 (NIV)

~ Fearing No Evil ~

"Yea, though I walk through the valley of the shadow of death, I will fear no evil: for thou art with me; thy rod and thy staff they comfort me." ~ Psalm 23:3-4 (KJV)

One night I dreamed I had gotten lost. Pulling my car to the side of the road, I fumbled in my purse. When I looked up, I discovered my vehicle was blocked by demons with evil, smirking faces.

I called a friend for help, and she appeared in my dream. We ran out of the car dodging the enemy. Periodically we even enjoyed our camaraderie as we successfully eluded our opponents. Desperately we searched for a place to hide but couldn't find shelter. There was nothing we could do, and all hope seemed lost.

Then I remembered verses from Psalm 27. As the enemy gradually and devilishly approached, I began saying the words of the Psalm. "Lord, you are my Light and my Savior, so why should I be afraid of anyone? The Lord is where my life is safe, so I will be afraid of no one! Evil people might attack me. They might try to destroy my body. Yes, my enemies might attack me and try to destroy me, but they will stumble and fall. Even if an army surrounds me, I will not be afraid. Even if people attack me in war, I will trust in the Lord." ~ Psalm 27:1-3 (ERV)

Immediately I sensed a power and stood confident in the authority of God's word. At that moment, I was released from the dream.

Even in my dream I realized my mistake. In a real-life situation I wouldn't have just called a friend, I would have called the police. Answers to problems and help for spiritual warfare will not come from friends, our thoughts, or our own strength.

Only a relationship with God can truly protect. Friends can support, pray, advise, and love us; but only God is our answer.

Only through God will our heart be kept from fear when the armies of hell besiege us. Only God has the power to break through evil, and God's word is power. Only God has the absolute knowledge to guide and protect, for only a Savior can save

"He is the only God, the One who saves us. To him be glory, greatness, power, and authority through Jesus Christ our Lord for all time past, now, and forever. Amen." ~ Jude 1:25 (NCV)

Mining for Treasure

Are you in a difficult situation? Call out to God.

Friends, family members, pastors, and those in ministry can join you in prayer, but make sure you personally pray for God's help. God is The One with the power to save.

~ Narrow-Minded ~

I've been pondering verses on the narrow road and the narrow gate. The verses give me pause because it's easy to talk about God's love, grace, and mercy, but much harder to think of those who are traveling the wrong roads.

I'm not being narrow-minded when I tell you there is only one way to heaven and that way is through Jesus. When I share Jesus, it's because I'm open-minded to making sure all know the offer of grace and mercy through the love of Jesus.

The world says there are many ways to heaven leading to many opportunities for a blissful ending. Yet Jesus says to come through the narrow gate. The road to destruction is broad and many go that way. But the small gate and the narrow road leads to life and only a few find it. Let's be the ones who find it and show others the way to the way!

And that narrow way, the one and only way to heaven, is Jesus. Jesus is the way, and the truth, and the life. No one comes to the Father except through Him (John 14:6).

If Jesus isn't the cornerstone of your faith, your faith is unable to save you. Without the heart of Jesus, beating in your heart, your heart is not safe.

Time is short and the door does not stay open forever. You do not have a guarantee you can wait.

Someone asked Jesus, "'Lord, are there just a few who are being saved?' And He said to them, 'Strive to enter through the narrow door; for many, I tell you, will seek to enter and will not be able. Once the head of the house gets up and shuts the door, and you begin to stand outside and knock on the door, saying, 'Lord, open up to us!' then He will answer and say to you, 'I do not know where you are from.' Then you will begin to say, 'We ate and drank in Your presence, and You taught in our streets'; and He will say, 'I tell you; I do not know where you are from; depart from Me, all you evildoers.'" ~ Luke 13:23-27 (NASB)

There are many who claim to be a Christian, but talk is cheap and even works are not an indication of salvation. "Not everyone who says to Me, 'Lord, Lord,' will enter the kingdom of heaven, but he who does the will of My Father who is in heaven will enter. Many will say to Me on that day, 'Lord, Lord, did we not prophesy in Your name, and in Your name cast out demons, and in Your name perform many miracles?' And then I will declare to them, 'I never knew you; depart from Me, you who practice lawlessness.' ~ Matthew 7:21-23 (NASB)

Not one person can ever be good enough. Jesus says in Mark 10:18 "No one is good except God alone."

Thankfully John 3:16-17 gives us the key to God's grace, "For God so loved the world, that He gave His only begotten Son, that whoever believes in Him shall not perish, but have eternal life. For God did not send the Son into the world to judge the world, but that the world might be saved through Him."

With that offer of grace, eternal life, salvation and entrance into Heaven, comes a beautiful loving revealing relationship. "He who has My commandments and keeps them is the one who loves Me; and he who loves Me will be loved by My Father, and I will love him and will disclose Myself to him." ~ John 14:21 (NASB)

Wouldn't it be narrow-minded of me if I didn't share what I believe about Jesus and His saving grace?

Please don't allow the enemy to lull you into complacency. Just because many people travel different roads, don't believe those roads will lead to heaven. Being "good" is not enough. Attending church or belonging to a certain type of religion is not all you need. Choose the narrow way. For the narrow way, the only safe place, the only way is by giving Jesus your heart.

And when Jesus comes into your heart, you are enveloped in His amazing, wonderful love. And God's love is anything but narrow, His love is free for all who come and is exceedingly, abundantly, more than you could ask or imagine!

When you travel the narrow way, your heart is opened to eternal, open-ended, free-flowing, unfailing love.

Mining for Treasure

Don't be narrow-minded, share the full wonderful truth of the love of Jesus Christ!

~ *Graveled Knees* ~

In my childhood I enjoyed riding my bike and loved the freedom of feeling the wind in my hair as I rode the neighborhood streets. When a new school was built near our house, the parking lot of smooth, black, asphalt beckoned. Full speed ahead, I peddled my bike across the lot.

Then my foot slipped.

The bottom bar kept me upright, but both knees hit the pavement. No hand brakes were available, and although I wrestled for control, all I could do was hold on for dear life. By the time I came to a stop, both my knees looked like hamburger meat embedded with gravel. Years later, scars remain.

Life's trials and difficulties tried to scrape off the skin of my soul. My past had many difficulties. I've been molested by a baby sitter, raped, chased by a man with a knife, drugged and locked up, divorced, stalked, eleven years of chronic illness, numerous surgeries, and a many other extremely unpleasant events. I wrestled with God over deep questions about evil and suffering. God's love patiently answered through His word as He healed, restored, and renewed.

Christianity doesn't mean we receive a pain-free life, however being a Christ-follower grants a beautiful eternal life. And God always causes all things to work together for good to those who love Him and are called according to His purpose. That's a promise.

God's earthly rescues may not always come the way we hope or imagine. Sometimes rescue comes swiftly, and other times come through healing of the broken-hearts and the binding of graveled knee wounds. Through the long and hard road of pain and suffering, God's gentle touch comforts, strengthens, and provides restoration.

And in the trials God reveals great and unsearchable things, because God never wastes a moment of our pain. Never.

Wounds come to us all. However, I can assure you if God doesn't take you around a difficult situation, His Divine Protection will take you through those difficulties. And our wounds will receive the grace-filled, loving touch of The One wounded for our sins.

"He heals the brokenhearted and binds up their wounds." ~ Psalm 147:3 (NASB)

"Even though I walk through the valley of the shadow of death, I fear no evil, for You are with me; Your rod and Your staff, they comfort me." ~ Psalm 23:4 (NASB)

Mining for Treasure

Do you have internal wounds that you wonder will ever heal?

God's healing touch is available no matter how terrible or deep the suffering.

~ *Cries of the Suffering* ~

The cry...

My soul is weary with sorrow; strengthen me according to Your word. Remember Your word to Your servant, for You have given me hope. My comfort in my suffering is this: Your promise preserves my life. My soul faints with longing for Your salvation, but I have put my hope in Your word.

My eyes fail, looking for Your promise. When will You comfort me? Though I am like a wineskin in the smoke, I do not forget Your decrees. How long must Your servant wait? If Your law had not been my delight, I would have perished in my affliction. I will never forget Your commandments, for by them You have preserved my life.

Save me, for I am Yours; I have sought out Your precepts. I call with all my heart; answer me, O LORD, and I will obey Your decrees. I call out to You; save me and I will keep Your statutes. I rise before dawn and cry for help; I have put my hope in Your word. My eyes stay open through the watches of the night, that I may meditate on Your promises.

Hear my voice in accordance with Your love; preserve my life, O LORD, according to Your laws. Look upon my suffering and deliver me, for I have not forgotten Your law. Defend my cause and redeem me; preserve my life according to Your promise.

May my cry come before You, O LORD, give me understanding according to Your word. May my supplication come before You; deliver me according to Your promise. May my lips overflow with praise, for You teach me Your decrees. May my tongue sing of Your word, for all Your commands are righteous.

May Your hand be ready to help me, for I have chosen Your precepts. I long for Your salvation, O LORD, and Your law is my delight. Let me live that I may praise You, and may Your laws sustain me.

God's answer...

Those who dwell in the shelter of the Most High will rest in the shadow of the Almighty. I Am your refuge and fortress, the One you can trust. Surely, I will save you from the snare and from the deadly pestilence. I will cover you with My feathers, and under My wings you will find refuge; My faithfulness will be your shield and rampart.

You will not fear the terror of night, nor the arrow that flies by day, nor the pestilence that stalks in the darkness, nor the plague that destroys at midday. A thousand may fall at your side, ten thousand at your right hand, but it will not come near you. You will only observe with your eyes and see the punishment of the wicked.

If you make Me, the Most High, your dwelling I Am your refuge—then no harm will befall you, no disaster will come near your tent. For I will command My angels concerning you to guard you in all your ways; they will lift you up in their hands, so that you will not strike your foot against a stone. You will tread upon the lion and the cobra; you will trample the great lion and the serpent.

Because you love me, I will rescue you, I will protect you, for you acknowledge my name. You will call upon Me, and I will answer you; I will be with you in trouble, I will deliver you and honor you. With long life I will satisfy you and show you My salvation.

I will be with you always, even until the end of this age. Don't be afraid, for I am with you. Don't be discouraged, for I Am your God. I will strengthen you and help you. I will hold you up with My victorious right hand. For I am living among you. I am a mighty Savior. I take delight in you with gladness.

With My love, I will calm all your fears. I will rejoice over you with joyful songs. As you love and obey My Son, Jesus Christ, you will always have My love, and your heart will be My home forever.

Based on Psalm 119:28, Psalm 119:49-50, Psalm 119:81-84, Psalm 119:92-95, Psalm 119:145-149, Psalm 119:153-154, Psalm 119:169-175, Psalm 91, Matthew 28:20, Isaiah 41:10, Zephaniah 3:17, John 14:23

Mining for Treasure

Are any of the verses above the cry of your heart?
Do you find comfort in the section of God's answer?
The Bible is a source of comfort and hope for every circumstance in your life. Take the time to find the treasure that waits for you.

~ Hand-Picked! ~

You are hand-picked. Yes, you!

You have been hand-picked to show how to live a hope-filled Christian life even in the midst of heartaches, trials, and suffering.

Hand-picked to bring joy to the joyless.

Hand-picked to show your scars, the hidden and visible wounds that Christ healed, to nurse and comfort a wounded world.

Hand-picked to make that phone call, to write that letter, to love on your babies, to tend to your family, to work in that difficult environment.

Hand-picked to crawl through each and every day of life's messes with your Savior to deliver a hope-filled message to those trapped in hopeless life.

Nothing about you is a mistake. You were lovingly hand-made and hand-picked by a loving God to be you. You are hand-picked and so very loved by the God of the universe. Hand-picked, and chosen, to shine the light of God into a world of darkness.

You, sweet, wonderful you, are hand-picked and chosen!

"For you have been chosen by God himself—you are priests of the King, you are holy and pure, you are God's very own—all this so that you may show to others how God called you out of the darkness into his wonderful light." ~ 1 Peter 2:9 (TLB)

"You did not choose me, but I chose you." ~ John 15:16 (NIV)

"For he chose us in him before the creation of the world to be holy and blameless in his sight. In love he predestined us to be adopted as his sons through Jesus Christ, in accordance with his pleasure and will—to the praise of his glorious grace, which he has freely given us in the One he loves." ~ Ephesians 1:4-6 (NIV)

Mining for Treasure

Read the following verses and remember you are loved and hand-picked by God!

"Before I formed you in the womb, I knew you, before you were born, I set you apart..." ~ Jeremiah 1:5 (NIV)

"You made all the delicate, inner parts of my body and knit me together in my mother's womb. Thank you for making me so wonderfully complex! Your workmanship is marvelous—how well I know it. You watched me as I was being formed in utter seclusion, as I was woven together in the dark of the womb. You saw me before I was born. Every day of my life was recorded in your book. Every moment was laid out before a single day had passed. How precious are your thoughts about me, O God. They cannot be numbered!" ~ Psalm 139:13-17 (NLT)

Always remember, you are formed with love by the God of the universe, hand-picked to be on planet earth at this very time, to be loved by the God of the universe.

~ Exploration ~

A job opened for a move to Idaho in 2009, and our family traveled 1500 miles to our new home. We were pretty clueless about the state when we arrived. Sure, we knew Idaho potatoes, but we didn't know Idaho.

So, Saturday mornings we traveled the roads enjoying the beauty of the state. Everywhere we went pictures were taken to capture the splendor of towering mountains, rushing rivers, deserts, and deep canyons.

Our road trips usually took all day, but to be honest, I don't think we went much farther than a few hours from home. I'm the one to blame. I'd make my sweet husband stop the car so I could jump out and take another photo. If there was a place by the river to sit and play in the water, well that was just too fun to ignore.

I don't want to miss anything, because in the exploration, discoveries are made, captured, and enjoyed. Sometimes there are hard journeys, winding roads, and mountains to climb before finding something worthwhile.

Life has joys, but also many hardships. At times I wondered if my life journey would be worth the effort. Mountainous trials, suffering, heartache, and pain led to many questions. As I've explored those difficulties with God, He has granted answers, comfort, wisdom, guidance, and healing.

Don't hesitate to talk to God about anything. Don't miss the exploration, because God's guidance is there for every step of the way, and no question is too big for our BIG God.

Mining for Treasure

What do you need to explore with God?

~ Vaulting Over the Fence ~

When our son was younger, he played baseball. During one game I overheard the pitcher and catcher discussing that they planned to hit the next batter. The next batter was our son.

And I tell you, I can be mild-mannered, kind, and gracious, but the thought of Scott getting hit just about had me vaulting over the fence. The momma bear in me was ready to pounce! However, sometimes the Holy Spirit cautions us to wait and trust.

Thankfully Scott wasn't hit, and I am grateful God kept me from grabbing those kids and winding up on the nightly news about an out-of-control mom.

We have an enemy. Satan is busy trying to steal, kill, destroy, and intimidate everyone he can. Fortunately, God vaulted over the bounds-of-eternity-fence to rescue mankind trapped in a fallen world. Jesus is our rescuer, redeemer, and Savior. There is no circumstance or situation too big for our Savior.

No matter what you face, no matter how the enemy is messing with your life or the lives of your loved ones, remember Jesus vaulted over the fence to fight for you. And God always fights for His children!

Mining for Treasure

Consider the following verses and take hope that no matter what situation you face, God won't every leave you, and His might and power are bigger than anything and anyone.

"The Lord will fight for you; you need only to be still." ~ Exodus 14:14 (NIV)

"For the Lord your God is the one who goes with you, to fight for you against your enemies, to save you." ~ Deuteronomy 20:4 (NASB)

"The Lord defends those who suffer; He defends them in times of trouble. Those who know the Lord trust Him, because He will not leave those who come to Him." ~ Psalm 9:9-10 (NCV)

~ *Be A Carrier* ~

"Four men arrived carrying a paralyzed man on a mat. They couldn't bring him to Jesus because of the crowd, so they dug a hole through the roof above his head. Then they lowered the man on his mat, right down in front of Jesus. Seeing their faith, Jesus said to the paralyzed man, 'My child, your sins are forgiven.'" ~ Mark 2:3-5 (NLT)

These men didn't just throw a prayer over their shoulder for their friend. They took action and responsibility. They didn't just carry their friend to Jesus; they dug through the roof to make sure their friend received help.

Will you do the same?

Will you carry your friends in prayer to the Savior?

Will you carry the lost in prayer, and in your actions, to help them find grace and mercy through Jesus?

When someone is sick and suffering, will you carry them to The Great Physician?

Let's be carriers, digging deep with faith, to help those who need Jesus.

Mining for Treasure

Does someone come to mind that needs your prayers and your help? How can you care for them today?

Take the time right now to carry them to the Lord in prayer. And if God impresses on your heart to do more, do so, and as you bless, you will be blessed.

~ Lost but Found ~

I was contemplating all the things I've lost in my life. There were many losses that shook my world causing me to grab for a firm faith footing. Yet then I thought of all the ways God has restored or replaced what the enemy tried to kill, steal, or destroy. I have lost much, but in Christ I have found everything.

Lost innocence, found restoration.
Lost income, found ever-lasting riches.
Lost loved ones, found unfailing love.
Lost homes, found eternal home.
Lost friends, found The True Friend.
Lost what was wasted, found all that is needed.

There is nothing I have lost that God hasn't replaced in amazing ways.

Whatever you have lost, all can be found in Jesus Christ.

"More than that, I count all things to be loss in view of the surpassing value of knowing Christ Jesus my Lord, for whom I have suffered the loss of all things and count them but rubbish so that I may gain Christ." Philippians 3:8 (NASB)

Mining for Treasure

What have you lost in life, yet gained in Christ?

~ *The Tale of The King* ~

Once upon a time, in a time far, far away, a child was born. The wild, evil, and ruthless tried to stop this child from ascending to the throne. Heartache, illness, pain, and suffering lined the dusty roads. But nothing can keep a King's child from their destiny.

You see The King sent His Son to pay the price for the world's sins and to open the doors to all. The ending has been written, and King's children always have a happy ending.

The amazing thing is, the story is true. And we make the choice to be in the King's family. And if we choose to be in His family, we receive every right and access of birth children.

If man wrote the tale, I picture raffles to compete for the top spots and only the best and brightest would be chosen. I wouldn't have a chance—I'm not that intelligent and my athletic skills are definitely lacking.

Fortunately, God's love and compassion is far above any human reasoning. The only requirement is an open heart to believe and receive His Son.

Jesus Christ has open arms waiting. Will you choose to be a child of The King?

"See how very much our Father loves us, for he calls us his children, and that is what we are!" ~ 1 John 3:1a (NLT)

Mining for Treasure

How different would you live your life if you knew the ending? What if you knew that no matter what came your way, you would have a place of safety and joy forever? If you have Jesus Christ as your Savior, you can be assured you have a place in God's heavenly kingdom.

And in heaven, the only tears will be shed from pure happiness—deep, belly joy laughter that makes you double over in delight.

"And God shall wipe away all tears from their eyes; and there shall be no more death, neither sorrow, nor crying, neither shall there be any more pain: for the former things are passed away." ~ Revelation 21:4 (KJV)

~ *Don't Miss the Marvelous* ~

As I read Psalm 118:23, "This is the Lord's doing; it is marvelous in our eyes", my eyes opened to see, feel, touch, and experience the marvel of the blessings granted by God. And in that moment the grandness of our God came clear.

Yet then I wondered, how often do I forget to marvel at God's magnificent creation, His children, His provision, and His wonderful works?

How often do I miss seeing what the Lord has done? How often do I miss the marvel of the moment? Unfortunately, the answers to my own questions are heartbreaking. I don't often stop and stand in awe at all God has created and all He has done.

I don't want to miss the best moments of life. I don't want to arrive in heaven only to discover I didn't enjoy all the amazing blessings God granted while I was here on earth.

Even in the trenches of the hard, messy, and uncomfortable of life, we are empowered to live fully immersed in the marvelous, because our marvelous Savior lives within us.

Open our eyes Lord, open our hearts, open our minds, and open every part of us to see and proclaim all that You are and all You do. Please don't let us miss the marvelous magnificence of You!

Mining for Treasure

Where can you see God's marvels? Read the following verses and note how you can watch for and experience the marvelous.

Declare (publish) his glorious deeds among the nations, Tell everyone about His marvelous works (1 Chronicles 16:24)

Sing to the LORD a new song, for he has done marvelous things! (Psalm 98:1)

You are a chosen race, a royal priesthood, a holy nation, a people for God's own possession, that you may tell everyone His excellencies who called you out of darkness into his marvelous light (1 Peter 2:9).

~ *Buried* ~

When I was a teenager, our family adopted a little dog someone had dumped on our country road One morning we offered him leftover biscuits. He took one look, scooped them in his mouth, walked around the house, dug a hole, and promptly buried the food. Even though those biscuits were great, I'm not sure they were ever retrieved.

I wonder how often we read God's word, or listen to a good sermon, and do nothing more than bury the truths? Growth as Christians won't come unless we apply and digest what we learn. James warns us not to be only hearers and not doers. We aren't saved to only sit in church services; we are saved to carry God's truth to a lost and hurting world.

When we feast on God's truth, we are given the opportunity to feed others. We are blessed to be a blessing. What is given is to be shared with others. Jesus suffered, died, was buried, and rose again to give us new life.

For those of us who have received the salvation of Jesus Christ, let's make sure we share the truth that couldn't be buried – the beautiful, amazing, blessings of God's grace!

"Go therefore and make disciples of all the nations, baptizing them in the name of the Father and the Son and the Holy Spirit, teaching them to observe all that I commanded you ..." ~ Matthew 28:19-20 (NASB)

Mining for Treasure

How can you apply God's truth to bless others?

~ *Letting Go* ~

During a time of prayer, I sensed God beckoning me to let go. And as I pondered what that meant, I realized there were things I had been holding tight, things that weren't the best.

The only thing I want to hold tight is to hold tight to my Savior. So, I realized what I needed to release into God's hands.

Let go of earthly vision to view God's vision.
Let go of every hindrance to be unhindered and available to God.
Let go of ideas to be open to God's ideas.
Let go of plans to be available to God's plans.
Let go of the past to be free from the past.
Let go of the hurts to heal.
Let go of bitterness to be joyful.
Let go of the worry and anxiety to have the peace of Christ.
Let go of fisted hands so open hands can be filled.
Let go of rights to be right with God.
Let go of self so self can be filled with God.
Let go of thoughts on how things should work, to allow God to work in ways exceedingly abundantly more than asked or imagined.

Heavenly Father I'm letting go of all of me so that You may fill all of me. I'm letting go to live free in You.

Mining for Treasure

What do you need to let go and release to God?

~ *White-hot Prayers* ~

One night I dreamed I was praying with several people and not one of them was paying attention to my prayers.

Then I <u>really</u> prayed, heart-felt, passionate prayers, begging God for His help. And immediately lives were changed before my very eyes. I woke and pondered how often I pray half-hearted prayers.

How often are results not accomplished or unseen, because of the lack of our passion and consistency with our prayers? James tells us "The earnest (heartfelt, continued) prayer of a righteous man makes tremendous power available [dynamic in its working]." ~ James 5:16b (AMP) And the King James Version says "The effectual fervent prayer of a righteous man availeth much."

The Greek definitions for effectual, fervent, and availeth means to put forth power, to be hot, to boil, to glow, to be strong, to have power as shown by extraordinary deeds, to exert, wield power, to have strength to overcome, to be a force.

I don't want my prayers to be weak and ineffective. I long for prayers that are powerful, white-hot, an overcoming strength, a force of God's power.

Throughout the Bible and throughout history, prayers have routed enemies, saved lives, and altered the destiny of nations. Holy and exalted, God loves us enough to give us the amazing blessing of conversing with Him. God who created the universe, the God who finds nothing impossible, listens to prayers. What will you ask Him? Will you come before Him humbly with prayers that are soul-deep and passionate?

Always remember "the effectual fervent prayer of a righteous man availeth much."

Pray, friends. Pray!

Mining for Treasure

I love this quote by Dawson Troutman on prayer, "Do you know why I often ask Christians, 'What's the biggest thing you've asked God for this week?' I remind them that they are going to God, the Father, the Maker of the Universe. The One who holds the world in His hands. What did you ask for? Did you ask for peanuts, toys, trinkets, or did you ask for continents?"

Now how will you pray?

"Ah, Sovereign LORD, you have made the heavens and the earth by your great power and outstretched arm. Nothing is too hard for you" ~ Jeremiah 32:17 (NIV)

~ *The Homecoming* ~

The last few years have blessed me with many opportunities to wonder about my life span. Illness, trials, surgeries, moves, and questions without answers, have kept me close to God. What if He is calling me home?

What if He is coming back to get us all this week? What if He is calling you home today? Would you be ready?

Going home with Him is the ultimate move -- no packing, custom made room or mansion, friends and relatives and the body of Christ already there. Paul reminds us in Philippians 3:20 that our citizenship is in heaven.

Before anyone knew we were coming to this world, Jesus has been preparing rooms in His Father's house for us! (John 14:2) He knows exactly what we like, what we need, and what we want. And no packing or unpacking needed.

And the best part, when we arrive home, God and Jesus will be there! Friends and family who have gone before will be there to show us around. Even if you've never had a homecoming party, you will get the ultimate home-coming!

God is watching, waiting, loving and longing for you. Please come home. A beautiful celebration waits. Tell others so they too can come home. If I get there first, I'll still be thinking of you all, loving you all, cheering you on, watching and waiting for you. Home is waiting!

"At the end of our meandering, up-hill-down-hill journey there is a loving Father waiting at the end of the pathway that we tread; watching, waiting, with open arms to welcome us back home... 'The Father's greatest joy is his children coming home.'" ~ Jack Brewer

"And I heard a loud voice from the throne, saying, 'Now God's presence is with people, and he will live with them, and they will be his people. God himself will be with them and will be their God. He will wipe away every tear from their eyes, and there will be no more death, sadness, crying, or pain, because all the old ways are gone." ~ Revelation 21:3-4 (NCV)

Mining for Treasure

Will you be part of the homecoming? I so want to see you in heaven! Let's rejoice together when we arrive safely home.

"For the Lord himself will come down from heaven with a commanding shout, with the voice of the archangel, and with the trumpet call of God. First, the believers who have died will rise from their graves. Then, together with them, we who are still alive and remain on the earth will be caught up in the clouds to meet the Lord in the air. Then we will be with the Lord forever." ~ 1 Thessalonians 4:16-17 (NLT)

~ About the Author ~

Lisa Buffaloe is a happily married wife, mom, and author. Lisa's difficult past experiences bless her with a backdrop to share God's amazing love. God's love is unending and through Jesus Christ we find healing, restoration, renewal, and the unfailing treasures of God's grace and mercy.

Please visit Lisa at...lisabuffaloe.com

Books By Lisa
(Updated July 2023)

Fiction
The Masterpiece Beneath
Nadia's Hope (Hope and Grace Series, Book 1)
   Prodigal Nights (Hope and Grace Series, Book 2)
   Writing Her Heart (Hope and Grace Series, Book 3)
   The Discovery Chapter (Hope and Grace Series, Book 4)
   Open Lens (Hope and Grace Series, Book 5)
The Fortune
Grace for the Char-Baked

Non-Fiction
Float by Faith
Heart and Soul Medication
Time with The Timeless One
The Forgotten Resting Place
Present in His Presence
We Were Meant for Paradise
One Lit Step: Devotions for your journey
The Unnamed Devotional
Flying on His Wings
Unfailing Treasures

No Wound Too Deep for The Deep Love of Christ
Living Joyfully Free Devotional, (Volume 1)
Living Joyfully Free Devotional (Volume 2)

Thank you for reading

Unfailing Treasures

Lisa Buffaloe

www.ingramcontent.com/pod-product-compliance
Lightning Source LLC
Chambersburg PA
CBHW070548050426
42450CB00011B/2761